By the same author:

The Whole World Is Watching
A Choice of Heroes
Listening to Midlife
A House Divided
Leading through Conflict

GLOBAL CITIZENS

How our vision of the world is outdated,
and what we can do about it

Mark Gerzon

RIDER

LONDON · SYDNEY · AUCKLAND · JOHANNESBURG

3 5 7 9 10 8 6 4 2

First published in 2010 by Rider, an imprint of Ebury Publishing

Ebury Publishing is a division of the Random House Group

The Random House Group Limited Reg. No. 954009

Addresses for companies within the Random House Group can be found
at www.rbooks.co.uk

A CIP catalogue record for this book is available from the British Library

The Random House Group Limited supports The Forest Stewardship
Council (FSC), the leading international forest certification organization.
All our titles that are printed on Greenpeace approved FSC certified
paper carry the FSC logo. Our paper procurement policy can be found at
www.rbooks.co.uk/environment

Mixed Sources
Product group from well-managed
forests and other controlled sources
www.fsc.org Cert no. TT-COC-2139
© 1996 Forest Stewardship Council
FSC

Printed and bound in Great Britain by CPI Mackays, Chatham ME5 8TD

Designed and typeset by Jerry Goldie Graphic Design

ISBN 978-1-8460-4217-1 (hardback)
ISBN 978-1-8460-4218-8 (paperback)

Copies are available at special rates for bulk orders. Contact the sales
development team on 020 7840 8487 or visit
www.booksforpromotions.co.uk for more information

To buy books by your favourite authors and register for offers visit
www.rbooks.co.uk

This book is dedicated to my family –
the whole family.

Contents

Acknowledgements

For the past decade, early versions of this manuscript circulated under the title *Leading Beyond Borders: A Handbook for Global Citizens*. I received detailed responses from readers around the world, and I thank them for their encouragement and criticism.

For the past twenty years, the board members and colleagues of Mediators Foundation have continued to inform and to support my work. Under the auspices of the Foundation, many of the global projects that have shaped my understanding of global citizenship – such as the Entertainment Summit in the 1980s, the Common Enterprise in the 1990s, and the Global Leadership Laboratory and Conflict Transformation Collaborative in recent years – have emerged and flourished. In particular, I appreciate colleague Simon Fox's wide-ranging support at the Foundation, and board member John Steiner's thoughtful responses to numerous drafts of this book over the past decade.

Four other institutional affiliations have helped to forge my global citizenship over the years. First, my experience as Managing Editor of *WorldPaper*, one of the first truly global newspapers, opened my eyes to the diversity of global perspectives. Second, the opportunity of leading the Global Partners team at the Rockefeller Foundation enabled me to experience the challenge of aligning diverse perspectives into action. Third, my years consulting with the United Nations Development Program, in particular the Bureau of Crisis Prevention and Recovery, taught me profound lessons about leading beyond borders in key nations around the world. Fourth, my tenure as a Distinguished Fellow at the EastWest Institute, which included working with my colleague Dale Pfeifer to build a network of global policy institutes from every region of the world, greatly expanded my understanding of both 'global thinking' and 'Track II' diplomacy.

In addition, I have consulted with a number of international organizations which provided me with unparalleled opportunities to witness global citizens in action around the world. I am grateful to all of them, including the Civic Exchange, the International Leadership Association, the Institute for Educational Leadership, the New Israel Fund, Outward Bound International, Search for Common Ground, the State of the World Forum, Synergos Institute and its Bridging Leadership Task Force, United Nations Leadership Academy, the World Economic Forum and the World Social Forum, among others.

As I now translate this book into action, I am working with a circle of colleagues to design and implement a Global Citizen Experience, a practical and highly interactive 'action learning' workshop that enhances global awareness. To all of these colleagues, who are inspiring me to new understandings and insights, I express my heartfelt gratitude.

So many colleagues and friends deserve my appreciation – for reading drafts, for introducing me to sources and interviews, and for educating me about their cultures – that I do not know where to begin. So I will simply say a collective 'thank you' to all of you here, and promise that a copy of this book inscribed with a message to you will be my personal way of letting you know that this is a much wiser book because of you.

Two thoughtful and committed women directly helped make this book a reality: my agent Jill Kneerim in Boston and my editor Judith Kendra in London.

I also want to thank my own multi-cultural family for inspiring me to write this book. In so many ways, we are a microcosm of the global family: a Cherokee-African-Mexican-

Polish-Ukrainian-Dutch-American clan that includes a mixture of Buddhist-Christian-Hindu-Jewish heritage. As we deal with our personal and cultural differences, we are discovering new dimensions to our relationships that have enabled me to understand global citizenship more deeply, and more personally.

Finally, I want to thank the woman I married thirty-six years ago, Rachael Kessler, for helping me learn to see her – and myself – as whole. In ways that are still mysterious, that has helped me see the whole world more clearly.

Mark Gerzon
Boulder, Colorado

Are You a Global Citizen?

I am a citizen of the world.

— **Diogenes Laertius, Greek philosopher** (AD 220)

The world is my country, all mankind are my brethren, and to do good is my religion.

— **Thomas Paine, American revolutionary** (AD 1776)

I am not a citizen of the world. I think the entire concept is intellectual nonsense and stunningly dangerous!

— **Newt Gingrich, American politician** (AD 2009)

Two millennia ago, philosophers in ancient Greece were already proclaiming themselves 'citizens of the world'. More than two centuries ago, American revolutionaries were declaring, 'My country is the world.' Over the past few generations, this visionary identity has been evoked by renowned political leaders (Mahatma Gandhi), endorsed by some of the greatest scientists (Albert Einstein), and even put to music (John Lennon). Clearly the idea of global citizenship is a deep and enduring part of human culture.

But here is the paradox: *legally*, none of the almost seven billion population of the planet is actually a citizen of the world. To my knowledge, no one carries a viable global passport; every one of these documents is issued by, or approved by, nation states.

So every one of us, including you and me, embodies this paradox: we are and we are not global citizens. Strictly speaking, none of us is a global citizen. Yet our only hope is to think and act as if we are.

Haven't we all been personally affected by the terrorist attacks of 2001 – or by the British and American responses to those attacks? Haven't all our finances been affected by the global economic crisis of 2008 – and the response of other countries to it? Aren't almost all of us concerned about the growing environmental crisis, including the threat of climate change, the health risks from breathing pollutants and ingesting contaminants in our food and water, etc.?

The truth is that we are *all* profoundly affected by the decisions and actions of people whose faces we may never see, whose language we may not speak, and whose names we would not recognize – and they, too, are affected by us. Our well-being, and in some cases our survival, depends on recognizing this truth and taking responsibility as global citizens for it. Whether the problem being debated is the financial crisis or immigration, war in the Middle East or the next pandemic, we human beings are now being challenged to realize that we are something more than citizens of separate nations, members of different races, and followers of different religions. We are also global citizens.

● ● ● ● ● ● ● ● ● ● ● ● ● ● ●

🌐 Tong Shan University. Zhuhai, China. May 2008.

'Why do the people in France hate us?' a Chinese student, one of almost three hundred seated in the large lecture hall, asked me. 'They tried to attack the Olympic torch when it was passing through Paris. Is that because they don't like our country? Is it because they are angry that we are a rising power?'

For a moment, I was speechless. I knew the answer to the Chinese student's question. So, I imagine, do you. The demonstrators were angry about the Chinese government's crackdown on Buddhist monks in Tibet, and more generally about its violations of human rights.

With the Beijing Olympics only a few months away, however, my Chinese hosts had specifically asked me *not* to talk about Tibet on this ten-day book tour that they were hosting. They worked for a government-managed publishing house that had just translated my most recent book, *Leading Through Conflict*, into Mandarin, and they did not want me to stir controversy.

For that instant, which seemed like an eternity, I could not decide what to say. Do I violate my host's request and jeopardize the rest of the trip? Do I assert that their government is at fault? Or do I sidestep the question?

'Before I answer,' I said, 'let me ask you all a question. In the current conflict between China and Tibet, there are two common ways of looking at it. One is that the violent behaviour of Tibetan demonstrators is the problem; the other is that Chinese policies are the problem. If you think *Chinese* government policy is the problem, please raise your hand.'

In the entire auditorium, there was not a single hand in the air.

'If you think the *Tibetans* are the problem, please raise your hand.'

A wave of hands shot into the air until the room was filled with a sea of fingers.

''Thank you,' I said. 'Now I want to tell you that a few months ago, at a university in the United States, I asked the same question. In that room, the results were just the opposite. Every single American student felt China was responsible for the bad situation; no one felt it was the Tibetans' fault.'

The students sat in shocked silence. It was incomprehensible to them that their American counterparts could see the Tibet–China conflict so differently from them.

'Do you think that classes like these where everyone thinks exactly the same will provide the best education?' I asked.

'No!' echoed around the room.

'Do you think that diverse opinions will make you smarter and make your country safer?'

Loud shouts of 'Yes!' formed a Chinese-accented chorus.

'I agree with you,' I said, building on their energy. 'China is a great country. Your power is rising. So you need to see *all* sides. When a wall of mistrust exists between China and another country, don't stop at the wall. You must use your minds, and your hearts, to see beyond it.'

● ● ● ● ● ● ● ● ● ● ● ● ● ● ● ●

Just as these students consider themselves to be 'Chinese', so do most of us have a national or cultural identity. Rarely do we think of ourselves as truly 'global'. Yet on every other level – genetic, physical, social, economic, ecological, technological, political and religious – we certainly are. Let's look briefly at each of these eight levels.

1. Our genes are global. Our genes define with amazing scientific accuracy our family tree all the way back to the beginning of *Homo sapiens* in Africa. Genomic research can easily establish exactly who our ancestors are and where they came from. Our genes prove that we are one human family, and that all of us are related. As the activist rock musician Bono gingerly asked a US audience: 'Could it be that all Americans are ... "African-Americans"?[1]

2. Our bodies are global. If we investigate the origins of the food we eat, or the medicines we take, we quickly discover that many of the ingredients are not local. Except in a few remote areas, most of our diet is not home-grown. Furthermore, the air and water on which we depend for our survival – while it may seem local when we breathe or drink it – are part of ecosystems that cross all boundaries.

3. Our societies are global. When we observe the communities in which we live, we no longer exclusively see people who look like us. Our neighbours or

co-workers, our children's classmates, the people we pass as we travel to work – they are becoming more and more diverse. They come from other places and other cultures. In some of our communities, they come from all over the world.

4. Our economies are global. When a financial crisis strikes, as it did most recently in 2008, the shock waves are global. Not just in one country, but in scores of nations around the world, stock markets plummet. The value of the money in our pockets is determined as much by the global currency market as by the actions of our own national government that printed it. Chances are high that our jobs, and certainly our children's careers, will depend increasingly on the global economy.

5. Our environment is global. The warming climate, the loss of forest land and the increase in erosion, the acidification of the oceans, the scarcity of fresh drinking water – these are global trends. We cannot protect our air, water, soil or food supply with only national environmental protection policies. Ultimately, we need environmental policies that transcend national borders.

6. Our possessions are global. Almost everyone lives in a dwelling, or rides in vehicles, or has possessions, which contain components that were made outside the borders of their own country. We can test the accuracy of this statement simply by looking at the things we own. The clothes I am wearing, the computer on which I write this sentence, the watch on my wrist – all of these artefacts were made outside the country where I live.

7. Our civic life is global. There is no country on the face of the Earth whose politics is not influenced by forces outside its own borders. This is true in giant nations like China, Russia, or the United States, and in small ones like Singapore, Nepal, Kosovo, or Rwanda. Today our 'internal', national political debates are more frequently than ever before shaped by 'external', international factors.

8. Even our religions are global. The beliefs we hold (or which, perhaps, we have rejected) have been formed and re-formed over many centuries, and through many cultures. Whatever faith one may call one's own – Christianity, Islam, Judaism, Buddhism, Hinduism, or other smaller traditions – it is very unlikely that it started where one lives. It is much more likely that it began far away, in another country, another culture, or even another continent.

So even if we are legally *national* citizens, every other dimension of our lives underscores that we are, in fact, *global* citizens. Narrow, exclusive human identities have reached a dead end. As separate nations, separate tribes and clans, separate faiths and ideologies, we created the problems we now face. Our vision of the world – divided along ethnic lines, national borders, and religious categories – is outdated. To update it, we must realize that the future is here, and it is global.

This shift of worldviews begins with Einstein's counsel: 'We cannot solve problems at the same level of awareness that created them.' So even as we pledge our loyalty to different nations, carry different currencies, serve in opposing armies, and follow different leaders, we must shift our level of awareness to include what is global. Split apart into diverse, sometimes clashing cultures, glib platitudes about 'oneness' and 'Spaceship Earth' are just not enough. Being a global citizen is neither a cool, ready-to-wear eco-identity, nor a chic lifestyle that we adopt by turning down our thermostats, listening to certain rock stars, eating locally grown foods or driving a hybrid, or even writing a cheque to feed a child or free a political prisoner. Although all these activities may be worthwhile, none makes us global citizens.

The breathtaking photographs taken by the first generation of early astronauts triggered an idealistic outburst of 'global awareness'. Biologists asserted more boldly that the Earth is a 'living organism' or 'Gaia', physicists described an 'unfolding co-evolution', theologians evoked a 'sacred Creation', and philosophers proclaimed an 'indivisible oneness'. As the futurist Arthur C. Clarke predicted optimistically, the 'more extreme forms of nationalism' would not survive now that we 'have seen the Earth in its true perspective as a single small globe against the stars.'

Unfortunately, however, the heady thrill of viewing our Earthly home from outer space did not instantly transform human consciousness. Instead, those beautiful portraits of our terrestrial home have been pushed aside recently by other images: the World Trade Centre in flames, conflicts in the Middle East descending into chaos, and ethnic violence from Kenya and the Congo to Sri Lanka and Kashmir. Tribalism, ethnocentrism, and nationalism have not disappeared; in many parts of the world, they are reasserting themselves. The seamless, interconnected world that brought the astronauts to tears is the same world in which Israelis and Palestinians fight over a small hill in Gaza; in which Tamils and Sinhalese massacre each other in a struggle for their small island of Sri Lanka; in which scores of countries with widespread hunger spend lavishly on weapons, and in which rich countries erect higher walls and tighten security to keep out poor immigrants.

What is needed now is a practical, results-oriented approach to global citizenship that meets Einstein's challenge. As so many global businesses are discovering, thinking globally is no longer idealistic. It is immensely practical. In globally competitive industries, a multinational company that fails to become a 'globally integrated enterprise' will not survive for long.[2]

● ● ● ● ● ● ● ● ● ● ● ● ● ● ● ●

University of British Columbia. Vancouver, Canada. November 2007.

'Contrary to the view of Tom Friedman,' says Mansour Javidan, referring to the *New York Times* columnist, 'the world is *not* flat. Maybe it will be seventy-five years from now. But now, the global cultural terrain is pretty bumpy.'

I am sitting here on campus with Professor Javidan; we are participating in a meeting of the International Leadership Association. I wanted to talk personally with this Iranian-born professor (who describes himself as a 'Russian-Iranian mix with an Arabic name') because he knows more than anyone about how 'bumpy' the world can be. In 1994, he formed a network of scholars around the world that he calls a 'United Nations of Academia' for the purpose of developing a truly cross-cultural research methodology. With his more than a hundred colleagues, he launched the GLOBE project, which has analysed the cultural differences that prevent us from truly learning – and leading – across boundaries.

'Every society has put a lot of energy into teaching its members to learn about people like them,' Javidan tells me, between sips of his very strong coffee. 'Now on a massive scale people have to deal with people who are different from them. In the world we are dealing with right now, people are increasingly dealing with people who are different from them. Never in human history have we experienced such massive-scale short-term contact across cultures.'

'Do you think we can cope with this?'

'Yes,' Javidan answers directly. 'But we will need a global mindset to do it.'[3]

• • • • • • • • • • • • • • •

Aware of this challenge, the global citizens from all over the world who you will meet in the following pages are not only creating a more just and peaceful world. They also are deepening the meaning of their lives. Global citizenship is both an 'inside' and an 'outside' job because the inner work of raising our awareness enables us to act in the world in more effective, transformative ways. When we truly understand our inter-connectedness, we realize that caring about the welfare of 'humanity' or 'the planet' is also *self*-care.

Although global citizenship is more urgent and more relevant than ever before, the leaders who dominate the world stage are national figures working in their national interest, not global statesmen working in the planetary interest. A 2008 World Public Opinion Poll asked a global sample of twenty thousand people which leader on the world stage inspired their confidence. Not one – not the USA's George Bush, not China's Hu Jintao, not Russia's Vladimir Putin – gained widespread support.[4] Only *ex*-leaders, such as Nelson Mandela or Bill Clinton, receive wide respect when they are clearly working on behalf of causes that transcend the agendas of a single nation.

If genuine 'global citizens' are to rise into positions of leadership, they must make this identity more concrete, specific, and grounded in tangible daily actions. It can no longer just be an educational ideal ('We are developing a curriculum to ensure that every one of our students becomes a responsible global citizen,' one elementary school principal told me). It can no longer just be a corporate mantra for pumping up global sales figures ('When we promote executives to the senior level nowadays,' said one CEO of a high-technology company, 'we look for experienced global citizens.') Nor can it remain a vague, high-minded cliché. (Even *Global Issues for Global Citizens*, the tome recently published by the World Bank, never managed to define what a 'global citizen' actually is.)[5]

To shift our level of awareness from the ethnocentric to the geocentric, we must challenge ourselves to leave our comfort zone. Whatever narrow identity we were born into, it is time to step out of it and into the larger world. We can still cherish our own heritage, lineage, and culture, but we must liberate ourselves from the illusion that they are separate from everyone else's.

● ● ● ● ● ● ● ● ● ● ● ● ● ● ● ●

⊕ Dubai, United Arab Emirates. July 2007.

'My name is Mark,' I said, shaking hands with one of the Muslim journalists. Like me, he was attending a small meeting between Western and Middle Eastern TV news editors who were concerned about how the media's coverage had increased tension between the regions.

'Hello,' he replied in English, but with a heavy Arabic accent. 'I am Jihad.'

'I'm sorry,' I said quickly, unsure about what I had heard. 'I didn't catch your name.'

'*Jihad*,' he repeated more clearly.

'Good to meet you,' I replied before moving on and introducing myself to the other participants in the meeting. But I promised myself that I would seek out Jihad during a break to find out more about his name.

'It is actually not an uncommon name,' he told me later. 'I was born in the mid-Fifties, and many Muslim parents were drawn to this name.'

'Why did they pick *that* name?' I probed, still puzzled.

'My parents wanted their son to succeed, and to excel at school. "Jihad" roughly translated means "hard work" or "perseverance". That is what my parents expected of me, and so they gave me that name.'

'But how—?'

Jihad raised his hand and smiled. He knew what I was going to ask before the words had left my mouth.

'The word has been hijacked by the extremists,' he said. 'When I was born, it simply meant to be diligent, devoted, and willing to work hard to become the best you could be. Now, in some circles, it means to wage a holy war. But that is not the original meaning of the word at all. If anybody knows the difference, it's me!'

● ● ● ● ● ● ● ● ● ● ● ● ● ●

Ultimately, the challenge of global citizenship involves building a bridge that connects 'us' and 'them'. In the following pages, we will look closely at what makes global citizens so effective at working beyond the borders that divide most of humankind. As we become acquainted with them, we will discover that they have developed four capacities which, taken together, enable us to meet Einstein's challenge and shift our level of awareness. These four capacities each express themselves through parts of our bodies: eyes, minds, hearts, and hands.

Witnessing: *Opening Our Eyes*. The journey toward global citizenship begins when we open our eyes. As the Buddhist masters put it: 'right seeing, right intention, right action'. Once we begin to *see* the world, then we can learn about it, connect to others, and partner with them.

Learning: *Opening Our Minds*. Once we can envision the world, we naturally want to learn. We can sense how our mind's full range has been narrowed. We are not satisfied with whatever our own culture (or subculture) calls 'learning'. Instead, we recognize that we can embrace the world only if our mind, like a door, is opened. Only then can we cross the threshold to the other side.

Connecting: *Creating Relationships*. The mind alone is not a passport across borders. To bridge the divides that separate us from others, global citizens need to navigate rivers of feelings as well as thoughts. We need to open our hearts and connect to the hearts of others, creating relationships even with those who may be called 'enemies'.

Geo-partnering: *Working Together*. With our eyes, minds, and hearts open, we are ready to act. But global citizens soon realize that no one of us can build a bridge alone. We need a counterpart on the other side. Ordinary partnerships will not suffice because we need an ally who is different from us. We need to open our hands, reach out and take theirs, and work together.

The Conclusion highlights twenty different ways to help us develop these four core skills more fully – witnessing, learning, connecting, and geo-partnering. Taken together, these twenty strategies are a curriculum for raising our 'global intelligence'.

After a lifetime of work in this field, I believe that as a

species we face a choice about whether or not we will invest in developing our 'GI'. If we do not raise our collective, global intelligence, we may close our eyes and become blind; close our minds and become rigid; close our hearts and become callous; close our hands and become aggressive. History shows that we human beings have both the capacity to open our eyes, minds, hearts, and hands – and to close them. We have the capacity to build an interdependent, peaceful global civilization and to splinter and fragment into endless conflict. We can see the world narrowly, or broadly, depending on which parts of ourselves we are able to develop. Indeed, wherever we may live, the drama of the Earth itself is occurring within each of us.

If we are willing to open our eyes, minds, hearts, and hands, then every one of us can become a global citizen.

Yes, *everyone*.

Chapter **1**

Witnessing:
Opening Our Eyes

*The purpose of life is . . . to know oneself. We
cannot do so unless we learn to identify
ourselves with all that lives.*

— **Mohandas K. Gandhi**

*The first day or two we all pointed to our
countries. The third or fourth day we were
pointing to our continents. By the fifth day we
were aware only of the Earth.*

— **Sultan bin Salman al-Saud, Saudi astronaut**

When the National Aeronautics and Space Administration (NASA) announced Project Mercury in October 1958, it committed the USA to putting a man into orbit around the Earth. But NASA officials soon found themselves in a power struggle with the astronauts. The men who were rocketing into space insisted on having a window in their tiny capsule. But NASA engineers argued that, given the dangerous temperatures upon re-entry, it would be an unnecessary safety risk.

'We won't fly without a window,' the astronauts said.

'We can't allow you to create hazards that could endanger your safety,' the NASA executives replied.

Although the astronauts eventually won the argument, soon afterwards the next conflict emerged: cameras. The technical experts and safety engineers argued that cameras would add unnecessary weight and increase risk. But the astronauts countered that recording what they had seen was a vital part of their responsibility. What good was seeing the cosmos if they could not share it?

To the enduring benefit of all humanity, the astronauts prevailed again. Thanks to these men and women from scores of countries – what astronaut Rusty Schweickart called 'sensing elements for mankind' – we all became witnesses to planet Earth.

Since then, human beings have repeatedly conducted the same radical experiment on members of our own species. The subjects of the experiment were men and women, Russians and Americans, Arabs and Europeans, Christians and Muslims, Hindus and Jews. They were sent into space in the tip of a rocket; they orbited the Earth, sometimes walking in outer space. Then they looked at the Earth from their magnificent, awe-inspiring, global perspective. When they returned, they were interviewed about how they had changed – physically, psychologically, and spiritually. Their responses can teach us more than we ever imagined about how a true global citizen witnesses the world.

But before we listen to the astronauts, let us first acknowledge their foresight in asking for a window and a camera. This is the essence of witnessing: to commit ourselves to seeing the world around us clearly and to share our experience with others. Witnessing means more than just looking. It means becoming aware of the lens through which we are viewing the world. To change our worldview, we first need to become conscious of having one.

The astronauts insisted on a camera because photography also embodies the spirit of witnessing. Photographers around the world have yearning for high-quality camera equipment, including a full set of lenses, so that they can accurately capture all kinds of scenes: close-ups, action, wide-angle, flash shots, etc. As global citizens, we are like photographers in that the quality of our observation depends on the accuracy of our lenses. We now have the capacity to view the world through multiple lenses, including a *global* lens.

A profound shift in vantage point occurred when these space travellers no longer witnessed space from Earth, but rather Earth from space. On the lunar voyage, instead of reflecting on the beauty of the moon rising about the Earth, the astronauts were the first in human history to view an 'Earthrise'. For those of us bound by gravity to Earth, it is hard to imagine looking up at the moon on a warm, clear night and remember walking on it. Yet that is precisely what can happen to James Lovell when he is outside at night near his family's cabin on a lake north of

Chicago, far from the city lights. The command module pilot and navigator on the epic six-day journey of Apollo 8 in December 1968, Lovell sometimes gazes up the bright orb and is flooded with memories. 'When you see Earth from the moon,' he says, 'you realize how fragile it is and just how limited the resources are. We're all astronauts on this spaceship Earth – about six or seven billion of us – and we have to work and live together.'[1]

The shift in perspective is Earth-shaking. The Russian cosmonaut Valentin Lebedev was startled by the experience of looking down on Mount Everest, and having trouble locating it because it was so small. Wubbo Ockels from the Netherlands was disoriented because space, which had once seemed so distant, now seemed so close. 'It took only eight minutes to get there,' he said, clearly stunned that he reached beyond Earth's atmosphere faster than he could 'drive from our home to our children's school'.

In addition to the psychological change, there was often a miraculous spiritual transformation. For Muhammad Ahmad Faris, from Syria, Earth seemed 'indescribably beautiful with the scars of national boundaries gone'. For Rodolfo Neri-Vela, from Mexico, the experience in orbit heightened his sense of connection to all humanity and his commitment 'to enjoy, to share, our short lives as fully as possible'. For Yuri Glazkov, of the USSR, the unfathomable blackness of space filled him with gratitude for the blessings of Earth. He envisioned planet Earth as a loving and caring mother who had been 'limitlessly kind to us'.

'We have grown strong and powerful,' Glazkov observed sadly, 'yet how have we answered this goodness?'

Like Glazkov, many of these space explorers experienced a heightened desire to care for their planetary home. Pham Tuan, of Vietnam, returned to Earth wanting 'not just to love her beauty, but also to ensure that we do not even bring the slightest harm to our natural world'. US astronaut James Irwin recalled that the 'blue marble' of Earth seemed so fragile and delicate that he thought, 'If you touched it with a finger, it might fall apart.' After flying over the United States, bathed in a light and powdery snowfall, the Russian Aleksandr Aleksandrov summed up the sentiments of so many others: 'And then it struck me that we are children of our Earth. It does not matter what country you look at. We are all Earth's children, and we should treat her as our Mother.' Echoing his Russian counterpart, the Israeli Ilan Ramon appealed for 'peace and a better life for everyone on Earth'.

In addition to wanting to treat the Earth with greater gentleness and care, these veterans of space wanted to treat their fellow human beings in the same spirit. Boris Volynov recalls that he became 'more full of life, softer' and wanted 'to be more kind and patient with the people around me'. Entering Salyut, the space station in which he would live and work for six months, Valeri Ryumin recalls that all the residents said to each other: 'We are brothers. I am you and you are me.'

If these voices belonged to monks or mystics, they might not surprise us. But these are not tales of spiritual seekers on the banks of the Ganges or in secluded monasteries. They are the matter-of-fact accounts of engineers, pilots, and scientists. What inspired them to speak like philosophers of the sacred was the unprecedented experience of witnessing the whole. Looking through a global lens transformed them. 'During a space flight,' said the USSR's Boris Volynov, 'the psyche of each astronaut is reshaped.' Or, as James Irwin put it simply: 'Seeing this has to change a man . . .'[2]

For virtually all of them, a veil fell away. Now they could see the whole, not just the parts. Now they could truly *witness*.

● ● ● ● ● ● ● ● ● ● ● ● ● ● ●

🌍 Kargar Avenue, Tehran, Iran.
20 June 2009. 7:05 p.m.

Neda Agha Soltan, a philosophy student and aspiring musician, and her music teacher, Hamid Panahi, stepped out of a car not far from street demonstrations protesting fraud in the controversial presidential election. Suddenly, the sound of gunfire erupted, and Neda fell to the ground. She began bleeding from her chest, and then more blood gushed out of her nose and mouth. Lying on her back, surrounded by a crowd, she died in a pool of blood on the street.

Videos of Neda's murder spread through the Internet, and around the world. Concerned that the protest movement had found a martyr, Iranian authorities forbade any memorial services for her. Fearing a wider demonstration, Iranian security officials prevented her family from giving her a proper funeral.

In Farsi, 'Neda' means 'voice' or 'calling'.

● ● ● ● ● ● ● ● ● ● ● ● ● ● ●

On Earth, as in the heavens, we have new 'windows' through which we can witness the world. The whole planet, and everything that happens on it, is becoming more transparent. For this reason, the skill of witnessing is more in demand. Just as a doctor needs to become more skilled at diagnosing the whole person behind the symptoms, so do global citizens need to become more skilled at witnessing the whole world behind the headlines.

Witnessing is observing from a place of deep awareness and inclusive attention. When it occurs, time slows down. Walls disappear. Borders do not exist. People stop shouting and hurrying, and begin to listen. The world, in a phrase, begins to come together. Those who once considered themselves separate, or even opposed, find ways to connect.[3]

In 1962, when President John F. Kennedy announced his intention to put a man on the moon, this vision of one Earth was still in its infancy. On 4 July at Independence Hall in Philadelphia, JFK issued a powerful 'Declaration of *Inter*dependence'. He called on all Americans – and the citizens of all nations – to wake up to the global dimension of our lives and our wider responsibilities. Kennedy recalled a time before the founding of his country when the leadership challenge was to 'think continentally' by forging thirteen separate colonies into one nation. Now, Kennedy said, we have to 'think *inter*continentally'. Paraphrasing the Constitution, Kennedy said:

> Acting on our own, by ourselves, we cannot establish justice through the world; we cannot insure its domestic tranquillity, provide for its common defense, or promote its general welfare, or secure the blessings of liberty to ourselves and our posterity. But *joined with other free nations*, we can do all this and more.

As Kennedy already understood almost half a century ago, a globalizing world requires a different kind of citizen, who deals beyond borders.

When the Prime Minister of the United Kingdom, Gordon Brown, visited the John F. Kennedy Presidential Library in Boston a few years ago, the primary message of his speech was the necessity of global citizenship. Building on the principles outlined by the US Founding Fathers, Brown proclaimed 'another self-evident truth: that *we are all of us* – all throughout the world – *in*

this together . . . There is no other planet for us and our children
– we must cooperate to make our stewardship of this Earth
work.' [4]

During the half-century between Kennedy's and Brown's
speeches, generations have come of age surrounded by images of
the Earth from outer space. These images have become so com-
monplace that it is hard even to recall a world in which a tall,
skinny twenty-seven-year-old graduate student named Stewart
Brand would stand outside the main gates of Columbia University
selling protest badges with the message: *Why haven't we seen a
photograph of the whole earth yet?*

In the decades since Brand (founder of the *Whole Earth
Catalog*) protested about NASA's delay in releasing the photographs from the first orbital flights, much of humanity has seen
the images of our dazzling blue-green planet framed against a
dark universe.

If we truly open our eyes, we discover that we have the
capacity to see the world as a whole. In this sense, we are *all*
'astronauts' now. Digital Global and GeoEye, the two private
companies that supply visual imagery to Google Earth, can now
take us anywhere on Earth in a matter of seconds. We can
literally see almost every square metre of the Earth with our own
eyes – simply with the click of a key on our computer.

No wonder the ranks of global citizens are increasing exponentially: the vast majority of humankind has been born after the
first photographs of the planet from outer space were taken. But
being able to see globally does not, by itself, ensure that we will
think and act in the best interests of all humanity.

● ● ● ● ● ● ● ● ● ● ● ● ● ● ●

🌐 'Terrorist' Hideout. Near Baghdad, Iraq. August 2006.

Eager to help anti-occupation forces attack US troops, a branch of al-Qa'eda called the Islamic Army in Iraq posted an instructional video on a jihadist website. It showed buildings at Iraq's Rasheed Airport where the offices of US military officers were located. The video zoomed in for a close-up of the area and described how the building could be most effectively targeted with homemade bombs. It concluded by providing precise coordinates for aiming rockets at the foreign 'invaders'.

The program they used to target US troops was Google Earth.[5]

● ● ● ● ● ● ● ● ● ● ● ● ● ● ●

How we use this eye-opening technology depends entirely on who we are and how we see the world. Although from a satellite the Earth is one, from the ground it can still appear divided. As anyone knows who has dealt with border conflicts, we cannot 'wish away' the reality of lines marked with fences, barbed wire, and – all too often – soldiers with guns. We may 'dream that one day, in the not-so-distant future, borders between states will simply vanish from our maps and our minds,' says Ambassador Marianne Berecz from Hungary, who works with the Organization of Security and Cooperation in Europe (OSCE) to monitor peace in the war-torn Balkans. But until that day comes, Berecz wisely concludes, 'we have to do our utmost here on Earth to make the lives of its inhabitants not only more free and more open, but also more safe and more secure.'[6]

These competing worldviews – *we are one* vs *we are separate*

– are reflected in how we use the new 'geo-eyes' that our technology has given us. We can use Earth-mapping technologies from an altitude of 30,000 feet to drop bombs on villages where alleged 'insurgents' live and to target barracks of troops of 'infidels'. Or we can use them to identify natural resources or chart the best terrain for agricultural irrigation. We can use this 'superpower' to heal or to kill, to feed or to starve, to plant or to plunder. Our purpose is determined by what *kind* of citizens we are.

State-of-the-art computer mapping of the Earth is only one of many tools we have for seeing the 'whole'. Another tool for witnessing that previous generations did not have is the global public-opinion poll. In earlier eras, we could plead ignorance. 'We' could say that we did not know what was happening to 'them'. We could claim that we did not know how angry or hurt 'they' were. But today, for the first time in history, we have the wealth and technology to find out systematically what other people think. We have scientific data-gathering about how residents of our 'global village' feel about their neighbours. What is striking about this polling data is that, despite the great expense and effort, 'we' seem to have limited interest in learning how 'they' feel.

For example, highly reputable Western research companies, such as Gallup, have gathered clear evidence about Americans' poor hearing regarding the US's role in the world. Specifically, polls make clear that:

- Americans think far more positively about their country than does the rest of the world.
- Americans think their motives are much purer than does the rest of the world.
- An estimated seventy million Muslims dislike the United States and think the attacks on the World Trade Centre were 'completely justified'.[7]

Assuming this data is valid, the next question is: what do we do with it? Will we ignore this vital information – or will we pay attention and respond?

• • • • • • • • • • • • • • •

Barafu Campsite, Mount Kilimanjaro, Tanzania. July 2006.

Having reached 15,000 feet, we were preparing for the final trek to the summit the next day. Huddled in our blue mess tent, my Kenyan colleague Kimani Njogu and I surveyed the tired but committed trekkers in Outward Bound International's first 'Global Leaders Program'. We were both amazed that so many of them – four Muslims from different nations, four Americans, and half a dozen more from other countries around the world – had been able to reach this altitude.

Although we were all tired from our third day of intense climbing, Kimani and I decided to catalyse an after-dinner conversation. We asked each person to share what made this *global* expedition different from a one-nation or single-culture trek.

'Here I can discover what people from Afghanistan think of Americans,' said an emerging leader from one of the new democracies in Eastern Europe. 'How two countries feel about each other is brought down to the level of two people on a mountain.'

'I've learned a lot about other worldviews now, and I know what I need to do to understand them even more deeply.'

'What makes this different from the UN is that here we can't write anybody off,' said another. 'We know that we *need* each other.'

'None of us has a single identity – each of us has a multiplicity of them,' said one of the participants from the Middle East. 'Becoming aware of that gives us more ways to connect to each other.'

'When I look at my climbing partners, I don't think of the countries they come from,' said the young politician from the Philippines. 'I think of them as someone who was there when I needed them the most. We are three days away from any health-care facility. My life depends on you!'

'I'm noticing that no one is saying this is about reaching the summit of Kilimanjaro,' said one of the Outward Bound guides. 'Everyone here is focused on other people. The way I would put it is: "You will remember the mountain, but you will remember each other more." '

'Is there some way,' said one of the Muslim men, with tears in his eyes, 'that we can bring the whole world into our small blue tent?'

● ● ● ● ● ● ● ● ● ● ● ● ● ● ● ●

To witness the many levels of citizenship that are currently unfolding in the world today, let us use the analogy of computer software, which is continually being upgraded. Today, in almost every society around the world, five levels of 'civic software' are in operation.

Here is a chart which summarizes and simplifies these different kinds of citizens:

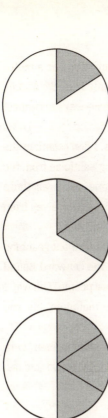

Citizen 1.0 –
Worldview based on one's self
(*egocentric*)

Citizen 2.0 –
Worldview based on one's group
(*ideocentric*)

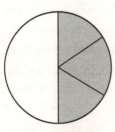

Citizen 3.0 –
Worldview based on one's nation
(*sociocentric*)

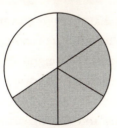

Citizen 4.0 –
Worldview based on multiple
cultures (*multicentric*)

Citizen 5.0 –
Worldview based on the whole Earth
(*geocentric*)[8]

At the most rudimentary level, **Citizen 1.0** looks out only for his or her own interest. It is 'egocentric' in that it is solely concerned with 'my' interests. Despite the negative connotations of the word 'egocentric', this most basic level of civic identity – based on one's own individual interests, needs, and attitudes – is necessary. But, alone, it is not enough.

In China, Peru and the USA, for example, I have worked with community leaders who are dealing with conflicts over water. When dams are built, the flow of irrigation to the surrounding farms is affected, and conflicts flare up because each farmer or rancher is fighting for his water supply. When too many citizens are only 'out for themselves', conflict is endless and often unproductive.

In all cultures, civic awareness naturally evolves to **Citizen 2.0**, in which the focus shifts from individual to group identity. Instead of thinking exclusively in terms of what personally benefits 'me', we think in terms of a larger 'us'. This group identity may be ethnic or tribal, or it may be embodied in a formal '-ism' of some kind (whether Catholicism or corporatism, communism or anti-communism). While their passports may indicate that they are Russian, or Brazilian, or Canadian, Citizen 2.0s in fact do not identify with the nation. They identify more with their particular subgroup than with the nation itself.

Seen positively, Citizen 2.0 is a widening of our identity so that we feel connected with others who are like us. Working within a framework of democratic institutions, these 'interest groups' represent the diverse elements of a society. Visit any nation and one finds these sub-national identities vying for control.

Not long after the economic and political crisis that devastated Argentina, I spent several days in Buenos Aires working with leaders of several political parties. I was struck once again by the universal paradox: they were all Argentineans who loved their country and were concerned about its future, yet each party's leaders were scheming against the others. Up close, every nation – from Nepal to Nigeria – is, to quote Abraham Lincoln, a 'house divided against itself'.[9]

When a nation is dominated by one of these 2.0 subgroups, the results can be catastrophic. At its worst, Citizenship 2.0 can lead to civil war, ethnic cleansing, and, if unopposed, genocide. Most of today's wars are civil wars, rooted in hatreds between competing groups that are defined by tribe, race, ethnicity, religion, or ideology. 'The explosion of communal violence is the paramount issue facing the human rights movement today,' concluded Kenneth Ross, acting executive director of Human Rights Watch. 'And containing the abuses committed in the name of ethnic or religious groups will be our foremost challenge for the years to come.'[10]

Precisely because of these dangers, we must upgrade our civic software to **Citizen 3.0**. Citizen 3.0 includes individual and group identities, but it transcends them in order to identify with a whole society or nation. At this level of awareness, citizens vow to defend the rights and interests of every other citizen of their nation, even if they are of a different tribe, party, race, or religion. Seen in its most positive light, 'nationalism' represents a widening of identity to include *all* of one's fellow citizens.

For example, an Anglo-Saxon British Citizen 3.0 who must deal with a Bangladeshi shopkeeper will consider that immigrant to be a human being of equal rights simply because he is a citizen of the United Kingdom. Similarly, a 'white' US President will celebrate the election of his 'black' successor because they are, no matter what their skin colour or ancestry, fellow Americans. Whether one is a Muslim Nigerian struggling to deal with the construction of a Christian church in the village, a secular Israeli trying to overcome stereotypes about an Orthodox neighbour, or a Canadian of English descent living in Toronto trying to deal with the influx of Asian immigrants, the challenge one faces is similar. It is to develop the inclusive national identity of Citizen 3.0.

However, in today's globalizing world, widening one's identity to include every other citizen inside that country's borders is no longer sufficient. As the twentieth century tragically illustrated, a unified nationalistic 'we' can demonize and attack a foreign 'them' and trigger world wars that leave civilization in ashes. 'Nationalism is an infantile disease,' said Albert Einstein prophetically in 1934. 'It is the measles of mankind.'[11]

For most of our parents' and certainly our grandparents' generations, most businesses were local; politics were primarily domestic; the media and entertainment were primarily national; daily life was geographically contained (except, of course, in times of world war). Today, most business is global; national economies are profoundly intertwined with the worldwide market; politics are dominated by international issues; and the mass media, largely through the power of the Internet, has become planetary. In such a world, the national consciousness of Citizen 3.0 is not enough. We human beings must evolve further because the whole simply cannot be managed by leaders who identify only with a part.

Citizen 4.0 represents a wider level of civic awareness because it breaks 'out of the box' of nationalism. For leaders and citizens who have developed this civic worldview, no single nation, religion, ideology, race, or ethnic group defines them. 'Cultural hybridization' is the word sociologists use to describe this phenomenon. 'Hyphens' is my slang equivalent.

'I am formed of the migrants who left Europe to find a new home in our native land,' said Thabo Mbeki, the former President of South Africa. 'I owe my being to the Khoi and the San whose desolate souls haunt the great expanses of [our land] . . . In my veins courses the blood of the Malay slaves who came from the east . . . I come of those who were transported from India and China . . . who were able to provide physical labour. Being part of all these people . . . I shall claim that . . . *I am an African.*'[12]

As a 'Khoi-San-European-Malay-Indian-Chinese' hyphen, who was leading a hyphenated nation, he did not identify with only one of those ingredients, but instead announced that he was all of them. Like golfing phenomenon Tiger Woods (who described himself as 'Thai-African-Cherokee-American'), Citizen 4.0s don't build bridges between cultures; they *are* bridges.

The cross-cultural awareness of Citizen 4.0 comes most naturally to those who do not belong to a single culture. They are 'outsiders' to every culture precisely because their biographies include experience in many. This exposure allows them to develop a multi-centric worldview that often conflicts with national perspectives.

After all his travels and interviews with heads of state, *Newsweek International* editor Fareed Zakaria says that people all over the world feel 'familiar' to him. But he does not credit his graduate education or his exposure at international conferences for this gift. Instead, he cites his multicultural background, which included both Western and Eastern education, and both Muslim and Christian family ties. What enables Zakaria to transcend an ethnocentric identity is his personal, intimate experience dealing with different cultures. 'There are many ways to develop a powerful feel for the world beyond America,' Zakaria observes, 'but certainly being able to feel it in your bones is one powerful way.'

As the globalization of culture accelerates, Citizen 4.0s who feel it in their bones are becoming more influential on the global stage. For a highly visible example, we need look no further than 1600 Pennsylvania Avenue. For more than two hundred years, the East Wing of the White House was occupied exclusively by white men and women of European, Christian stock raised in the continental USA. For the first time in history, beginning in January 2008, the President and First Lady came from a family that is black-white-Asian, Christian-Muslim-Jewish, and speaks English-French-Cantonese-German-Hebrew-Swahili-Luo-Igbo.[13] With this combined lineage, the current resident of the White House clearly has the capacity to witness deeply the world beyond his country's borders.

The number of Citizen 4.0s is growing rapidly because the vast majority of human beings are now living in more than one culture at a time. Recognizing multiple cultural realities is a vital step in the unfolding of civic consciousness. Some specialists in global education even state as their goal to 'prepare the next generation of students to embrace *multiple* loyalties . . . '[14] But Citizenship 4.0 is only a part of the path toward, in Gandhi's words, 'identify[ing] with all that lives'.

Citizen 5.0 takes us beyond the multicultural worldview and embraces not only all human culture but *all* of life. Citizen 5.0 is not multi-national, but *trans*-national. It is not limited to the human dimension, but recognizes that the foundation of all life, including human life, is nature itself. *Homo sapiens* is a guest in the home we call planet Earth, and our health, well-being, and prosperity ultimately depend on the host. Albert Einstein put the challenge of Citizen 5.0 most clearly when he said, 'Our task must be to free ourselves from this prison [of separateness] by widening our circle of compassion to embrace all living creatures and the whole nature in its beauty.'[15]

Indeed, it was this shift to Citizen 5.0 that often disoriented the astronauts. The rapid and abrupt exposure to the indescribable beauty and wonder of Earth's oneness triggered a 'leap' to this transcendent perspective. Their experience underscores that, no matter who we are, none of us is a complete stranger to even the widest and most inclusive identity. *Since all these worldviews are within each of us*, we have the capacity to relate to people everywhere.

On a planetary scale, learning to be 'advocates for the whole' means recognizing this ecology of worldviews as part of global civilization. To be a global citizen requires the wisdom and humility to deal with these competing loyalties:

- Citizens 1.0 can maintain singular loyalty to themselves.
- Citizens 2.0 must balance their self-interest against the interests of their group (clan, tribe, party, etc.).
- Citizens 3.0 must subordinate self and group loyalty to the interests of their nation.
- Citizens 4.0 have loyalties to multiple cultures.
- Citizens 5.0 must integrate all of the above into their loyalty to the Earth and all living things.

Global citizens, then, are compelled to face the challenge of competing loyalties that cannot be resolved by easy answers and quick, glib solutions. This is uncharted territory in which every person, every citizen, must face themselves. When loyalties conflict, as they inevitably will do, whom ultimately do we serve?

• • • • • • • • • • • • • •

🌐 Yangon, Myanmar [Burma]. September 2007.

A Japanese photographer, Kenji Nagai, is covering the protests by Buddhist monks and their supporters near the Traders Hotel, a few blocks away from the Sule Pagoda in the capital city of Yangon (Rangoon). Movie camera in hand, he is running to keep up with the demonstrators who are fleeing from government soldiers.

Suddenly, Nagai falls to the ground. Still holding his camera, he tries to lift himself off the road. But then he collapses back to the ground. Moments later, his limp body is carried away by men in uniform.

Autopsies reveal that a bullet entered from the lower right of his chest, pierced his heart, and exited from his back. The military government of Myanmar claim that his death was accidental, the unfortunate result of a 'stray bullet'. Critics of the Burmese dictatorship assert that he was killed in cold blood at point-blank range.

• • • • • • • • • • • • • •

If you have Internet access, you can see for yourself what happened to Kenji Nagai. Just go to YouTube, enter his name, and click. Watch the video and ask yourself: Was he hit by a 'stray bullet' as the government claimed? Or was the soldier standing over him, as he lay on the ground, firing at him at precisely the angle that corresponds to the autopsy report? Since you can see it with your own eyes, you can decide for yourself. You are no longer a second-hand news *consumer*. You can now be a *witness*.

'My friend J. had gone to work over in Burma,' says Ryan McMillen, a young assistant professor of English and history at

Santa Monica College in California. 'One morning soon afterwards, I received this email from J. in my in-box. It showed this photographer being killed.'

Standing on the rooftop of his apartment building, J. (who will remain anonymous for his own protection) focused his cell phone camera on a scene in the street below. Troops were leaping out of their vehicles and chasing demonstrators. J. shot a video of the street below, including the moment when the Burmese soldier fired at Kenji Nagai, dropping him to the ground. Still holding his heavy video camera, Nagai tries to raise himself up. But the final shot is lethal; he lies motionless until troops carry him away.

Shocked by what he had seen, J. emailed the video of the murder to a handful of trusted friends. Ryan was so haunted by it that he watched it repeatedly.

'It just kept bothering me,' Ryan recalls. 'I felt really torn. On the one hand, I was concerned about my friend's safety. On the other hand, I wanted to get this story out to the public.'

Ryan checked out the different news websites, and finally settled on CNN because he thought it had the 'easiest access'. He clicked on CNN's 'I-Report' link, where it advises: 'Use the toolkit to find out how to send video, photos, and audio from your computer or your cell phone.' Ryan posted J.'s explosive video on I-Report.

Thirty minutes later his phone rang. It was a CNN reporter who asked him some background questions and then decided to run the story. Within minutes, images of Kenji Nagai's death were being transmitted from Atlanta, Georgia through cyberspace around the world. Despite the Burmese government's desire to obscure this murder, two ordinary citizens – using only cell phones and laptop computers – broke the story wide open.

Shocked that the event that they had tried to censor had entered the global news cycle, the Burmese authorities did what dictators do best: they tried to kill the messenger. They cut off the Burmese people's access to the Internet. They were less concerned about the death of Kenji Nagai than about the way the new cybermedia had evaded their control. But they were too late. The message was already out. Within days, their claim that Nagai was hit by a 'stray bullet' was revealed for what it was: a bold-faced lie by dictators trying to hide their violent oppression of their own people.

Ryan McMillen then shared the video with another friend, a freelance journalist in Bangkok, who decided, as did CNN, that this story was hot. One of the publications that decided to run his story was the *Hollywood Reporter*. Eager to play up the local angle of the story, the editor plastered this headline across the top of the page of the October 4 edition: 'L.A. professor triggers Myanmar Web shutdown.'

> BANGKOK – A Los Angeles academic may have been a driving force behind the move by Myanmar's 19-year-old dictatorship to shut down Internet access after bloggers posted images of soldiers killing civilians. The images included footage of a Japanese photographer for APF News shot dead at point-blank range by a soldier chasing demonstrators.[16]

I did not learn about the story from either CNN or *Hollywood Reporter*, but from the *New York Times* delivered to my doorstep. There was a stock photograph of Kenji Nagai, whose murder in a city halfway around the world had become a part of my life – just as now it is part of yours.

'When your friend sent you the video clip,' I asked Ryan, 'did he know you would do something about it?'

'Yes, I think so,' Ryan replied. 'It just seemed like the right thing to do.'

But why did it seem like the 'right thing' to Ryan? *Because he had become a witness.*

As recently as twenty years ago, when the last round of protests rocked Burma, being a witness was much harder. Back then we would have had no proof that the government was lying, and the lie might have passed as the truth. 'It took days, sometimes weeks, even months to get images out,' recalls Aung Zaw, editor of the independent *Irrawaddy Magazine* and its companion website. 'Now, it's so fast. It's clear that the [Burmese] government views the Internet as an enemy.'

'This time . . . there are lots of new technologies to get the news out of Burma,' concurs Vincent Brossel, director of the Asia desk for Reporters Without Borders. 'People are able to take pictures, videos to evidence what is going on. It is quite amazing for Burma, which is a very poor country. Technology is the most useful weapon you can use in such types of pacifist struggles.'[17]

● ● ● ● ● ● ● ● ● ● ● ● ● ●

Mexico City, Mexico. October 1968.

Fifteen thousand students gather to demonstrate against the government in the main downtown square of Mexico's capital city. In the full light of day, the demonstration takes place with many innocent bystanders watching the confrontation between the students and the government troops.

The government claims that communist-inspired student provocateurs opened fire on the military, and in the ensuing battle, four people died. The protesters and other witnesses claim that the military launched a ruthless attack, massacring five hundred people and wounding two thousand.

● ● ● ● ● ● ● ● ● ● ● ● ● ● ● ●

When this student-led pro-democracy demonstration occurred in Mexico City, there was no Internet, no personal computers, no Web browsers, no cell phones with cameras. The massacre in Mexico City involved hundreds of deaths but was shrouded in mystery for decades. Forty years later, the murder of one man in Myanmar was revealed within twenty-four hours. Although plenty of witnesses were gathered in Mexico City, watching the protest from countless apartment buildings that formed the perimeter of the square, we have no substantial visual record of what they witnessed.

Without access to cyberspace, the world was too 'big' to witness its wholeness. Governments, particularly the more authoritarian ones, could attempt to control the information that was released to the outside world. But today communication technology makes that virtually impossible.

Radio was the first technology to bridge almost all borders, enabling our ears to receive news from around the world. Then, beginning with BBC broadcasts in 1936, television empowered our eyes. Unlike radio, which required fifty years to reach fifty million people in the USA, television reached an audience of that size in only thirteen years. After that, the pace accelerated exponentially. It took twenty years for the first billion cell phones to sell worldwide, four years for the second billion, and two years for the third billion. The World Wide Web required only six years to reach an audience of 100 million people. The weaving together of humanity into one communications matrix is accelerating to the point that these high-tech global media have changed the meaning of community. Today almost everyone – including villagers looking for work, tracking down a rural doctor, or deciding to which market to transport their farm produce – is connected.

Of course, even with this high-tech global set of eyes and ears, no one can see and hear *everything* that happens on Earth. But we can develop our senses so that we are increasingly aware, not only of what we see, but of what we would otherwise have missed. This is why the British musician and visionary activist Peter Gabriel founded Witness, a web-based hub for gathering and distributing video of human rights violations. With a bold tagline – 'See it. Film it. Change it.' – *Witness* spotlights videos like the one sent to Ryan McMillen.[18]

Digital media are the dictator's worst enemy because these technologies cannot be put in jail or killed. The World Wide Web enables the kind of boundary-crossing flow of information that dictators and tyrants hate. They do not want local knowledge to become global knowledge, but now they often simply cannot stop the news from spreading.

Today many 'watch' organizations are hard at work around the clock keeping an eye on the Earth for us. Human Rights Watch alerts us to defend those who otherwise might be undefended. Amazon Watch and the many other 'River Watch' networks around the world are collectively witnessing and protecting the world's most vibrant waterways. So are Vietnam Labor Watch (reporting on unfair and unhealthy working conditions), Australian Paper Watch (dealing with deforestation), Baikal Watch (monitoring Lake Baikal), and many others.[19] As the invisible becomes visible, the Earth comes alive before our very eyes.

Our 'geo-eyes' enable many of us to view the planet as if we were astronauts – but without going into orbit. Being able to 'see' our entire planetary home is an extraordinary and unprecedented opportunity – and, at the same time, a profound challenge for each of us as well. Whether it is the changing temperatures in the polar ice fields or the rate of deforestation in the Amazon rainforest, the number of prisoners in the Soviet Union or college graduates in South Africa, we can learn almost anything about the world with the click of a key on a computer. But with such an overwhelming amount of non-stop data bombarding our minds and hearts, will it make us more aware – or just numb?

'Can we have too much information?' asks Beth Anglin, the Director of Outward Bound's Peace Centre, who is concerned that the answer might be yes. 'There are many people I know who are global information junkies. They read so much. They also comment on-line, often anonymously, to protect themselves. But they do not take action or risk themselves in any way to make a positive impact.'

'But human suffering still touches them, doesn't it?' I asked her.

'Yes, but even for those who allow themselves to feel the pain of the world, the burden can be traumatic. I think we have a lot to learn about how to process all of this information in a way that enables the witness to move from being merely a *receiver* of information to becoming an active *participant*.'

The risk of information overload falls most heavily on the under-thirty generation in the developed world. Raised in the cell-phone, global music, news, and Web culture they have access to more information without leaving their at-home technology than exists in the most extensive libraries in the world. The advantage they have is that data is abundant; the danger is that, in the over-abundance, they lose the ability to respond.

● ● ● ● ● ● ● ● ● ● ● ● ● ●

🌐 A private home outside London, England. November 1956.

As Soviet tanks rolled into Hungary, the hopes of the Hungarian people for freedom were crushed. Determined to repel the Soviet invaders, Hungarian citizens of all ages joined the resistance. By the time the Soviet military regained control, more than twenty-five thousand Hungarians were dead and hundreds of thousands wounded or imprisoned.

At the height of the invasion, in early November 1956, the BBC carried vivid images of this resistance. One of the millions of viewers was a thirteen-year-old English schoolgirl named Scilla Elworthy.

'I was just playing around the house,' remembers Scilla. 'But then I noticed the images on the television. Children not much older than me were throwing themselves under tanks.'

Frozen, she watched in horror as ordinary citizens, unorganized and unarmed, sacrificed their lives in a valiant effort to prevent Hungary from falling under the oppressive control of the Soviet Union.

Outraged by the scene, thirteen-year-old Scilla marched upstairs and began packing her bags, intending to go to Hungary.

As soon as her mother discovered what Scilla was doing, she told her daughter to put her clothes back where they belonged.

'You're not going anywhere,' she said firmly. '*Pull yourself together, young lady.*'

● ● ● ● ● ● ● ● ● ● ● ● ● ●

'It was one of my mother's favourite phrases,' Scilla said recently, as she walked near her home in the Cotswolds. But to her credit, young Scilla refused to 'pull herself together'. She was unwilling to be a mere spectator sitting powerlessly in front of her television screen. Close to tears, Scilla told her mother that she could not go on playing as if nothing had happened. Slowly her mother realized that she was not witnessing a little girl's passing hysteria, but a deep and serious response to the injustice of the world (If you want to watch these images, just go to the Web.)[20]

'All right, Scilla,' her mother said, sitting down and taking her in her arms. 'I'll tell you what we can do. If you'll put your clothes away and settle down, I'll promise to help you learn the skills that you'll need to make a difference. Right now you're just too young to go. But if you prepare yourself – and I'll help you – you'll be able to do something about this when you're older.'

Calmed by her mother's words, Scilla began unpacking – and her mother kept her promise. In the next few years, Scilla went to work during her school holidays in a home for refugees from Nazi concentration camps, listening silently to their stories, and thinking about how such atrocities could be prevented. At nineteen, she worked in a camp for Vietnamese boat people in France, and translated that experience into a university dissertation on refugees. At twenty, she worked in North Africa during the Algerian revolution to house and care for children left orphaned by the violence. Later she created an innovative nutrition-education organization to combat starvation in southern Africa. Thanks to her fierce determination, and her mother's love, she turned her intense reaction to the injustice on the television screen into a lifelong commitment to be a witness to the world.

For billions of human beings, the television and computer screen have become portals for witnessing the world. How we respond depends on who we are. Our responses are personal, and they differ widely. Scilla's brothers and sisters did not react as she did, just as you and I might respond differently to any particular news story. But global awareness requires of each of us the capacity to be *moved* and to take 'response-ability' for our world. Without this capacity, 'global news' becomes nothing more than a sedative, and 'global awareness' just another mental abstraction.

On the one hand, we are part of 'webs' that connect us. But on the other, we are building 'walls' that divide us. Everywhere in the world, from the Kremlin to the White House, leaders are trying to cope with this intensifying webs-versus-walls dynamic.

A month after the terrorist attacks on the World Trade Centre and the Pentagon, President George W. Bush's three main speech-writers were drafting the speech that would define the approach that the USA would take in addressing the threat of terrorism. In one of the competing drafts, they wrote: 'In the long-term, terrorism is not answered by higher walls and deeper bunkers.'[21]

They wrote that sentence because the three men knew it was true. If we are imprisoned behind barricades or buried under-ground, we may obtain a measure of short-term 'security'. If we invest more and more in higher walls, barbed or electrified wire, guard posts, metal detectors, elaborate airport security systems, and other barriers, we may be 'safe' but we will also be blind. *And how safe can we be if we cannot see?*

Unfortunately, President Bush deleted the sentence about 'higher walls'. Instead, he told the world: 'You are either with us or against us in the fight against terror.' The White House declared a 'war on terror' and divided the world into 'them' and 'us' – a worldview that persisted in the US government for seven long, tragic years.

The walls we human beings build are reflections of our identities. They symbolize our attachment to an identity that makes us want to keep 'them' separate from 'us'. Because our ancestors lived in small tribes, they learned to build bonds of trust with the familiar faces of kin and clan. In most cultures, they learned to be wary of the stranger, the barbarian, the alien, the foreigner. In a frightening and uncontrollable world, it was sensible to build a wall between 'us' and 'them' for self-protection. The 'us' was just large enough to create a genetic pool, form hunting groups, and create a self-sustaining community that could keep 'them' at a distance.

In that tribal, us-and-them world, weapons could not strike farther than an arrow could fly; communication media could not reach farther than the sound of a drum; transportation was limited to four-legged creatures on land and canoes on water; and production methods that were simple and non-polluting. But in the postmodern world, weapons can radiate the entire biosphere; media can reach around the world; transportation enables us to be almost anywhere on Earth in less than a day; and industries are so toxic that their chemicals have entered the milk of our mothers' breasts and the bones of our children's bodies. In such a world, us-versus-them walls do not protect us. They endanger us.

As global citizens, the practice of witnessing can help us avoid this fateful mistake. Witnessing enables us to stop *projecting* onto the world our simplistic, black-and-white images of 'them' and 'us' and to start *seeing* the Technicolor reality. Since there are always external threats, the key to security is witnessing those threats accurately. If our hearing is weak, we cannot heed a warning. If our vision is blurred, we cannot identify the attacker. If we cannot witness, we are shooting in the dark.

● ● ● ● ● ● ● ● ● ● ● ● ● ● ●

🌐 **Private apartment. Beirut, Lebanon.
May 2008.**

Having returned to his hometown after being posted
abroad, Mohamad Bazzi watched nervously from his
apartment as young men loitered on the sidewalk outside
brandishing rifles and handguns. Fresh in his mind was
an incident from an earlier civil war when he and his
family violated one of the cardinal rules of urban warfare:
he went, unarmed, to the window. But the flutter of the
curtains caught the eye of the Hezbollah commando
across the street who 'swung his rifle toward our window.
It pointed directly at us . . . We scampered away from the
window, back in the hallway.'[22]

As Mohamad and his wife know all too well, to
approach the window during urban warfare is to risk
one's life. So first one steals quick glimpses through the
closed curtains. Then one may open the window and stick
one's head out for a brief glimpse. Only when a sense of
security returns does one dare to step out on the balcony
and actually look around.

● ● ● ● ● ● ● ● ● ● ● ● ● ● ●

This yearning to observe, even if it involves risking our lives, is
built in to the human organism. Even more than our ears and our
nose, our eyes are the key to our survival. This was true
hundreds of thousands of years ago when our species emerged
and began its great expansion around the world. And it is true
today as our species, rapidly heading toward nine billion souls,
imperils the planetary home on which we now depend.

Our ability to witness the whole, not just see the separate

parts – the original and fundamental unity, not just the fragmented and superficial human overlays – may well be the key to our survival. If we see parts, we will build walls; but if we can witness the whole, we will build bridges.

Only recently have behavioural scientists documented how profoundly culture shapes our vision. Just because all human beings have eyes does not mean that we all see the same thing. What we see depends in large part on what we are trained to look for.

Not long ago psychologists conducted an experiment with students at Kyoto University in Japan and Michigan University in the USA. On both campuses, subjects viewed a vignette of fish swimming. When asked what they had observed, both Japanese and American students naturally referred to the fish. But the Japanese made 60 per cent more references than their US counterparts to background elements in the vignette, such as water, bubbles, plants, etc., and this difference in observation reflects a profound cultural contrast between Asian and Western modes of perception. To oversimplify, Westerners tend to see separate individual objects ('figure'); Asians tend to see context and relationship ('ground').[23]

This example of cultural differences, chronicled in Richard Nesbit's provocative book *The Geography of Thought: How Westerners and Asians Think Differently – and Why*, is part of an avalanche of research that establishes how our culture shapes our vision. Along with other books with titles such as *Can Asians Think?* (by a Singaporean author) and *The Geopolitics of Emotion* (by a French author), this rapidly growing literature alerts us to the simple yet elusive truth that what we see, and how we interpret it, is conditioned by our upbringing. If we want to see globally and think globally, then we must learn something that our own culture alone cannot teach us.

This is particularly true for the nations that are 'superpowers' and can impact the entire world. The American presence in Iraq is a tragic example. If only American leaders had witnessed Iraq before invading it, they would have realized how different Iraqi culture is from others. Unlike America, Iraq is not a young nation 'discovered' by pioneers, but one of the oldest nations in the world. It was not created by a band of 'Founding Fathers' who forged a national identity together, and whose loyalty is to their national government in their capital city. On the contrary, Iraq is composed of tribes whose primary loyalty is to their local lineage group. In Iraq, there will never be the equivalent of a hall in Philadelphia where leaders form a national democracy by signing a 'Declaration of Iraqi Independence'. Democracy there will never be top-down. It will be bottom-up. And it will not look like an old version of America. It will look like a new version of Iraq.[24]

Unfortunately, the occupying armed forces, although highly skilled in military strategy, were profoundly ignorant about the culture they were invading. For example, in attempting to pacify the town of Fallujah, the foreign troops chose an elementary school as their interim headquarters, thus alienating every Iraqi family in the area with a school-age child.[25] Similarly, US troops created intense resentment among young men in Baghdad by eliminating several popular soccer fields in the process of building a $1.5 million Tigris River Park as a 'good will gift'.[26] As these examples indicate, *attacking* a country without first *witnessing* it is a prescription for disaster.

• • • • • • • • • • • • •

🌐 Indian Peaks Wilderness Area. Eldora, Colorado. July 2002.

With two quarts of water, rain gear, and a sketch pad in my backpack, I amble quietly through a high mountain meadow. The sound of a full, tumbling stream draws me toward it. I sit down and look at the glistening water cascading over boulders and rocks.

Too difficult, I think to myself. I can't draw water.

Then I look up at the mammoth mountain that dominates the southern rim of this valley. I try drawing the ridge line only.

Too big. Too massive. Too large a canvas.

Aware of my limitations as an amateur artist, I decide to forget about drawing and simply enjoy my hike. As I reach higher altitudes, the path grows steeper and my breathing deepens. Even the trees begin to thin out, unable to survive in thin air and powerful winds. As I pause for a drink of water on a promontory overlooking the valley, I notice a small pine tree. Rooted precariously between two boulders, it barely reaches to my waist.

Draw me! it says.

At first I resist its request. After all, surrounded by the magnificence of the Rocky Mountains, why would I want to draw this nondescript little tree? Back in the city, caught in the normal busy pace of my life, I would not have noticed it at all.

But when I finally decide to draw it, the tables quickly turn. As soon as my drawing pen hits the paper, this 'simple' tree becomes so complex, such a microcosm of the universe, that I am humbled. The lines that I begin drawing do not begin to capture the reality of this baby tree struggling to survive. So I pause and look again.

Branches angle off twisting in all directions. They are cloaked by thousands of nettles and sustained by an intricate web of invisible roots. Overwhelmed, I begin by outlining its branches' architecture. For the first time, I realize that it is far more developed on one side than the other. Within moments, this nettled professor is teaching me about the four directions, the position of the sun, the patterns of the wind, and the arc of shadow.

Slowly, my eyes awaken. I begin at last to really witness the tree.

● ● ● ● ● ● ● ● ● ● ● ● ● ● ●

If it is hard to witness fully even a single object, it is far harder to witness a complex culture – much less the whole world. No wonder we have great difficulty finding consensus about much more complex global issues, particularly if they reopen religious and ethnic wounds. From this perspective, we can have compassion when other people or other nations 'see' the world differently than we do.

Recognizing this reality is the first step. Rather than immediately trying to persuade others of our point of view, we can turn our gaze inward and become more aware of how our way of seeing has been shaped by our culture in ways that we do not even begin to understand.

Geographic boundaries are only one of the many dividing lines. Religious, national, ethnic, economic, cultural, and ideological borders all further fragment our vision and reduce us to competing, and often unconscious, 'worldviews' (otherwise called 'mental models' or 'memes').[27] If we develop the capacity to see the world as global citizens, as many of the astronauts did, we can become aware of these borders without identifying with them. But this requires something more than witnessing. It requires learning.

Chapter 2

Learning: Opening Our Minds

You can tell whether a man is clever by his answers. You can tell whether a man is wise by his questions.

— **Naguib Mahfouz, Egyptian author**

Education is the ability to perceive the hidden connections between phenomena.

— **Vaclav Havel, former Czech President**

A biased mind never sees the complete picture, and any action that results will not be in tune with reality.

— **The Dalai Lama**

I n order for me to write this book, and for you to read it, we both have to un-learn some of what we were taught as children. Most of us can never become global citizens unless we re-examine some of what we were taught by our own culture. All of us, no matter in what culture we were raised, inherit cultural, national, and religious belief systems. Unless we un-learn them, we inevitably project these worldviews onto the world.

The world is the actual territory. Our world*view* is our map of that territory. Having a worldview is not only reasonable; it is inevitable. The world is too complex and too vast to be comprehended in its fullness by a human mind. So we naturally create worldviews that reduce the complexity so that our minds can cope. When we resort to religious categories like 'Muslims' or 'Christians' or 'Jews' or national categories like 'Russians' or 'Iraqis' or 'Japanese' we tend to make the world simpler than it is. We pre-judge who they are, what they believe, where they live – and that 'pre-judice' distorts reality. Like the old Mercator maps that hang on many schoolroom walls and that distorted the surface area of the Earth, these culturally shaped worldviews often distort reality. We think we are looking at the world. But we are not. We are simply staring at our map of it.

Unfortunately, most 'learning' in the modern world fits the formulas of the culture in which it is being taught. Although it is natural to teach more about one's own cultural history, religious tradition, and political or economic ideology than about those of others, problems arise when we fool ourselves into thinking that this kind of partial education is comprehensive. Obviously it is not. Although learning about one's own part of the whole is a wonderful way for children to begin their education, the education of global citizens cannot stop there. If it does, we as a species are in trouble. *We cannot manage the whole Earth with citizens who have systematically failed to learn about parts other than their own.*

These partial worldviews represent a devil's bargain with our minds. Without knowing it, our minds shrink the world down to a manageable scale. By making the world fit our worldview, we can now more easily 'explain' it. We can construct a simplified narrative that, taken to extremes, makes us 'right' and them 'wrong', or makes us 'good' and them 'bad'. By drawing borders around our tribe or our nation, or around some other convenient 'we/they' construct, we no longer have to fully perceive the world. Inside the box of our own worldview, we reduce 'others' to stereotypes.

● ● ● ● ● ● ● ● ● ● ● ● ● ● ●

🌐 Bar. Downtown London. May 2007.

'These four guys were walking down the street, a Saudi, a Russian, a North Korean, and a New Yorker,' jokes my friend Arun. 'A reporter comes running up and says, "Excuse me, what is your opinion about the meat shortage?"

'The Saudi says, "What's a shortage?"

'The Russian says, "What's meat?"

'The North Korean says, "What's an opinion?"

'The New Yorker says, "Excuse me?? What's excuse me?"'

I laugh and take another sip of my beer. But I feel strangely uncomfortable.

'Here's another one I heard last week in Istanbul,' Arun continued. 'How many Frenchmen does it take to screw in a lightbulb?'

'I don't know,' I reply, even more ill at ease than before.

'One. He holds the bulb and all of Europe revolves around him.'

Even as we both laugh, I begin to understand my discomfort. Both of Arun's jokes are based, pure and simple, on stereotypes. I am wondering about my theory of humour when Arun jumps in again.

'A Texan farmer goes to Australia for a vacation. There he meets an Aussie farmer and gets talking. The Aussie shows off his big wheat field and the Texan says, "Oh! We have wheat fields that are at least twice as large." Then they walk around the ranch a little, and the Aussie shows off his herd of cattle. The Texan immediately says, "We have longhorns that are at least twice as large as your cows."

'The conversation has almost died when the Texan sees a herd of kangaroos hopping through the field. He asks, "And what are those?" The Aussie replies with an incredulous look, "Don't you have any grasshoppers in Texas?" '

● ● ● ● ● ● ● ● ● ● ● ● ● ● ●

What makes these jokes 'humorous'? It is the images in our minds of other cultures. These stereotypes are convenient because they simplify the infinitely complex. It's much easier to label people than to learn who they actually are. For this reason, most human beings are raised with a 'ready-to-wear' worldview that includes simplistic stereotypes of other cultures. Some of what we are taught is true; some of it is not. So part of the journey of global citizenship is to learn to tell the difference.

I remember the Sunday when I was twelve years old, and the minister of our church gave me a certificate with five stars on it. Each star represented a passage from the Bible that I had recited from memory. My mother was so proud of me that she bent over, swept me up in her arms, and took me to the local ice-cream shop where she bought me a large vanilla cone dipped in soft, warm chocolate. I was in sugar heaven.

I gradually understood, however, that what I was receiving from her was not love, but approval. The ice-cream cone was a reward for becoming a 'good Christian'. When my child-like memorization of the Bible morphed into adolescent enquiry, her praise disappeared.

'Will the children in China really go to hell because they don't believe in Jesus?' I asked her when I was thirteen years old, unable to believe what she had told me. She was in the basement folding laundry.

'Yes,' she replied without hesitation. 'In the Bible, Jesus says, "I am *the* way." '

'But that doesn't seem fair,' I continued. 'Chinese children have never been told about Jesus. Why should millions of innocent children be punished when they haven't done anything wrong?'

'It is not for us to question God's will,' she said sternly.

'But—'

'Asking too many questions is a sign of a weak faith.' She stood up, picked up the laundry basket, and went upstairs. At that moment I began to recognize the difference between the deep love of being accepted for who I was, and the cultural reinforcement for conforming to what I was expected to be. Her message could not have been clearer: if I asked too many questions, I would not only forfeit God's love, I might lose hers as well.

I thought of my mother when I returned not long ago from my fifth trip to China. I was amazed to realize that since I left home for college at the age of seventeen, I have spent more time in China than in Indiana, the Midwestern American state of my childhood. I have more close friends today among the Chinese 'heathens' than I do in the 'Christian' neighbourhood where I grew up. In fact, I work more closely today with my colleagues in Beijing and Hong Kong than with anyone in Indianapolis.

In retrospect, I understand now that my mother could not *witness* the world because she *projected* onto it. My mother was the daughter of Dutch missionaries who spent much of her childhood in Jogjakarta, Indonesia, where her father was the strict principal of a Dutch Reformed Church school. Early in her life, she learned that there were believers and non-believers; the saved and the damned. She held firmly on to this Christian worldview until a series of strokes destroyed this and other identities once and for all.

Because of my parents' journey – meeting on the island of Curacao where my mother, a teacher, and my father, a Dutch infantry lieutenant, was stationed; marrying and moving to the USA, where my father went to graduate school in chemistry at Cornell University – my passport records the fact that I was born in Ithaca, New York, in 1949. I therefore entered the world legally as an American citizen (not Dutch or Indonesian) and now, more than sixty years later, so I remain. But to become a global citizen, I had to let go of certain beliefs that I was taught as a child. Unless and until we release these un-truths, we remain trapped in narrow identities that prevent us from becoming whole.

● ● ● ● ● ● ● ● ● ● ● ● ● ●

1. Ellis Island, New York City. Spring 1949.

S. is a short, foreign-looking man with dark skin. Lodged in a first-class stateroom on an ocean liner after crossing the Atlantic, he enters the harbour, passing the Statue of Liberty. Dressed in suit and tie, speaking carefully cultivated English (he watches Hollywood movies, and has read Darwin and

Einstein), he is welcomed with professional courtesy. He has chosen America as a place to study because his home country, Egypt, has been in political turmoil. After spending some time in New York City, he travels by train to Colorado. In the small rural town of Greeley, S. attends classes at the Colorado State College of Education. After successfully completing his course of study, he returns to Egypt.

2. Los Angeles International Airport. January 2004.

T. is also a short, foreign-looking man with dark skin. T. arrives by aeroplane from Asia. He is wearing unusual clothing, speaks only rudimentary English, and is surrounded by young students in equally strange garb. Without warning, he is taken out of the immigration line, separated from his compatriots, and taken alone into a small room. Security guards go through every one of his belongings, including reading his personal letters. They search his body, and ask him to remove some of his clothing. They question one of his colleagues, a young monk who has a degree in chemistry, about whether he is knowledgeable about bomb-making. T. spends more than an hour being searched and interrogated to determine whether he poses a security threat to the United States of America before he is finally released.

● ● ● ● ● ● ● ● ● ● ● ● ● ● ●

The contrast between how these two men arrived in the United States of America could not be starker. In fact, one of them became a preacher of terrorism, while the other became a teacher of peace. It would be easy for us to assume that the one who arrived comfortably on a luxury ocean liner became a friend of America, and the one who was harassed at the airport become its enemy. *But the opposite is true.*

Paradoxically, S – Sayyid Qutb – was welcomed with courtesy, yet he grew to hate the USA, became an advocate of violence, and used his writing to inspire scores of 'terrorists'. On the other hand, T. – Thich Nhat Hanh – was treated like a terrorist and experienced the bombing and napalming of his home country of Vietnam by the US Army. Yet he developed a deep affection for the USA, became an advocate of non-violence, and was nominated for the Nobel Peace Prize by Martin Luther King, Jr.

What explains this paradox? Let's take a closer look at these two men in order to find the key difference, which is about how these two men *learned.*

Sayyid Qutb left the United States shocked by the sexual promiscuity of the West, and outraged by America's support of the 'Zionist oppressors' in Israel. During his entire time in the USA, he remained suspicious and ill at ease, particularly with women. Despite a warm welcome, he remained separate and distant from his hosts. In the white-dominated town of Greeley, Colorado, at a time of widespread racial segregation, the darkness of his skin and the intolerance of his host culture toward 'Negroes' made him resentful and afraid.

By the time he returned to Egypt, his negative reaction to the West had hardened. 'The white man in Europe or America is our number-one enemy,' he wrote. 'The white man crushes us underfoot while we teach our children about his civilization, his universal principles and his noble objectives . . . We are endowing our children with amazement and respect for a master who tramples our honour and enslaves us. Let us instead plant the seeds of hatred, disgust and revenge in the souls of these children. Let us teach these children . . . that the white man is the enemy of humanity, and that we should destroy him at the first opportunity.'[1]

For the rest of his life, Sayyid Qutb preached vengeance and violence as a political strategy. His writings inspired Ayman al-Zawahari, Osama bin Laden, and the other architects of al-Qa'eda to promote a wave of violence that continues to this day.

Called 'Thay' by his students, Thich Nhat Hanh is a Vietnamese monk. Because of his deep faith and his commitment to non-violence, he did not respond with hatred or anger to the US military's devastating impact on his country. Despite his disappointment about his rude treatment, Thay responded not with rage but with sorrow and compassion. 'Our way of dealing with terrorism is taking us down a dangerous path of distrust and fear,' he reflected following the experience. 'It is time to stop. Let us pause. It is time to seek *true* strength and security.'

In the workshops that he taught following the interrogation, including speeches to members of Congress on Capitol Hill, he explored the roots of terrorism. From his perspective, hating the 'enemy' was not the solution. It was the problem.

'Misunderstanding, fear, anger, and hatred are the roots of terrorism,' he said. 'They cannot be located by the military. Bombs and missiles cannot reach them, let alone destroy them, for terrorism lies in the hearts of human beings. To uproot terror, we need to begin by looking in the hearts of human beings.'

'Terrorism is caused by wrong perceptions,' Thay told his followers around the world. 'They have wrong perceptions of "us", and we have wrong perceptions of "them". Using bombs will not change those wrong perceptions. Radar cannot locate wrong perceptions. Only compassion can.'[2]

For his entire life, Thich Nhat Hanh has been devoted to non-violence, which led to his nomination for the Nobel Peace Prize. His spiritual community in France, Plum Village, has inspired thousands of students from all over the world.[3]

To understand the paradox of these two men with what Westerners might call 'strange' names, 'foreign' facial features, from 'far-away' countries is to begin to understand the difference between ordinary learning and *cross-boundary* learning. Both Thay and Sayyid received formal education, gave lectures, and wrote books. Both visitors were learned men, and were considered to be scholars in their own cultures. But the difference between the two men was the *borders* of their learning. Sayyid could only learn within the narrow confines of his own faith, culture, and ideology; Thich Nhat Hanh went beyond those borders and found empathy and compassion for others – even the people of the country that devastated his own country, killed many of his fellow citizens, and forced him into exile at the risk of his life. While Sayyid was unable to cross borders, Thay could – and that made all the difference in the world.

Nothing illustrates the freedom that comes with cross-boundary learning more clearly than the relationship of Sayyid and Thay to their respective faiths' traditions. Sayyid was a devout Muslim; Thay was a devout Buddhist. But the issue is not the difference in their faiths. (After all, there are 'narrow-minded' Buddhists and 'broad-minded' Muslims.) The issue is the *relationship* of their identity to their faiths. Sayyid turned his religious doctrine into a mental prison with the bars of his cell made out of beliefs, not steel. Thay turned his religion into a stairway toward fundamental, universal principles that allowed him to reach a higher plane from which all religions had value. *Sayyid turned differences into walls that divide; Thay turned them into bridges that connect.*

'I am a Buddhist practitioner,' said the Dalai Lama, in words which Thich Nhat Hanh would certainly affirm, 'but if I mix up my devotion for Buddhism with an attachment to it, my mind will be biased toward it. A biased mind never sees the complete picture, and any action that results will not be in tune with reality.'[4]

This capacity for cross-boundary learning is essential for all of us today, whether we are world leaders or ordinary citizens. It enables us to transcend the borders of our own identities and to learn from anyone, anywhere.

The borders that divide humankind are constructed first by our minds, and only second by many hands. These walls take many forms, both physical and political, visible and invisible. Sometimes, as in Israel, they are made out of cement; or, as between the USA and Mexico, metal and barbed wire; or, as in Berlin during the Cold War, of stone and brick. But behind the physical border is a mental one that has been reinforced with politics. Without the official document issued, you and I cannot move freely between most countries. A guard stands there, often armed. He will stop us unless we have documents that prove we are citizens of acceptable origin. We need the permission from their nation to cross the imaginary line that demarcates their territory from ours.

Notice in the following table five kinds of borders within which most of humanity has been raised – including you and me.

BORDER:	DEFINED BY:
Individual	Self-interest
Tribal/Racial	Group loyalty
Religious/Ideological	Orthodoxy
National	National interest
Corporate/Economic	Profit/market share

Most of us spend our lives within a combination of these borders. They shape our identities. They transform us from *Homo sapiens* into members of cultures, who see the world through an unconscious cultural lens. Unless we become aware of it, these borders can close our eyes, minds, and hearts to the rest of humanity.

My visit to Tong Shan University (described in the Introduction) reminded me that a generation of young people today, raised less by their parents' ideologies than by the Internet, are wrestling with this very issue. I was lecturing there in 2008 when a student near the back raised his hand, and I called on him.

'My question is not easy,' he said fluently in English. 'Why, Mr Gerzon, are stereotypes so hard to change?'

It was the end of a two-hour seminar, with over two hundred and fifty students in this cavernous lecture hall. I was amazed at their stamina, their curiosity, their determination to learn about the world. I wanted to give this young man a thoughtful answer, but to be honest, the question was so profound that I did not know what words in English would make sense to them. (They had asked me to speak to them in English, rather than use my translator.)

'What comes to my mind,' I said, trying to use the simplest vocabulary possible, 'is two words. The first word is *lazy*. The second word is *mind*. I think stereotypes are about lazy mind.'

I paused for a moment, checking to see whether I was being understood. I could tell from the expressions of the faces of the students that they were following me, so I continued.

' "The British" is a stereotype. So is "the Chinese". The British people are very different from each other. So are the Chinese. Isn't that true?'

Many of the students turned to each other, nodding. They knew exactly what I meant.

'In America, people speak of "Chinese food". This too is a stereotype.'

They laughed, so I decided to expand on this thought.

'In Beijing, I ate Mandarin-style food. Delicious. Then in Shanghai, I ate Shanghainese cuisine. Very different, also so delicious. Here in Zhuhai, I ate Cantonese dishes. Very different, and *most* delicious.'

They laughed again.

' "Chinese food" is a stereotype. Before, my mind was lazy. I believed the stereotype. Now, I know better. There are many kinds of Chinese food – and I love them all!'

To my surprise, they applauded because they were happy to know that this foreign visitor had begun to learn about the exquisite complexity of their traditions. So it seemed like an opportune moment to challenge them.

'If *you* want to change *your* stereotypes, seek first-hand experience. Do not believe everything you are told. Find out for yourself. Talk with someone from France. Talk to a demonstrator, or an activist. Talk with people who you do not understand. Your stereotypes will change – just like mine did.'

Because most of us were trained inside cultural borders and taught that they were real, our minds are not free. The hallmark of this kind of learning is what one business leader in Bahrain called the three R's: 'read, remember, and regurgitate'.[5] This is still the most widespread form of so-called 'learning' in the world today. The challenge of global citizens is to un-learn the half-truths that separate us and re-learn the deeper truths that connect us.

If we spend our entire lives 'learning' inside the cultural and national borders in which we were raised, we develop a colonized mind. The more we learn inside these boundaries, the more certain we become that our interpretation of the world is correct. Such 'inside-the-box' learning is relatively easy because its base is 'additive': it never requires that we question or 'let go' of anything we have learned. This kind of learning focuses on the acquisition of new skills, increased knowledge, additional degrees – in short, *more*. We can simply acquire more information without modifying our existing beliefs, or our current identity.

Cross-boundary learning, on the contrary, often requires *less*. Almost everyone says they want to learn more; but how many of us are willing to let go of the spectacles through which we view the world? Many leaders say they want to 'think globally'; but how many of us have the courage to stand up against the conventional wisdom of our own communities?

Unfortunately, this kind of ethnocentrism is the rule rather than the exception. Our so-called leaders, especially, often view global issues through the lens of their national education and make decisions today based on yesterday's realities. In an unstable, dynamic, globalizing world, this can be disastrous.

Consider for a moment any of the major issues that grab the world's attention. From the wars in the Middle East to the financial crisis, from climate change to terrorism, from religious conflicts to immigration – leaders in positions of power, usually between the ages of forty-five and seventy-five, make decisions based on attitudes formed when they were under twenty-five and living in their original culture. In terms of their innate 'reflexes' that are often triggered in times of crisis, most leaders are twenty to fifty years behind the times – and trapped in their own cultural mindset rather than thinking from a global perspective.

'Unfortunately, whether they are running corporations or foreign ministries or central banks,' observes Joshua Ramo, former foreign editor of *Time* magazine and managing director of Kissinger Associates, 'some of the best minds of our era are still in thrall to an older way of seeing and thinking. They are making repeated misjudgements about the world . . . We've left our future, in other words, largely in the hands of people whose single greatest characteristic is that they are bewildered by the present. The sum of their misconceptions has now produced a tragic paradox: policies designed to make us safer instead make the world more perilous.'[6]

India–Pakistan, Russia–Ukraine, China–Taiwan, Iran–USA, Israel–Palestine, Turks–Kurds – all of these relationships recently experienced significant challenges. Are the leaders dealing with these challenges in the present – or are they, too, many decades in the past? Are these leaders thinking globally as they face the current situation – or are they acting out narrow ethnic stereotypes or national biases that are generations old?

The US–Russia relationship is a prominent and explosive case in point. Locked for decades in a cold war, the 'American capitalists' and the 'Soviet communists' developed a fixed, negative view of each other. A relationship was formed based on fear, competition, mistrust, and a power struggle. I know this first-hand from my experience in the 1980s organizing an 'Entertainment Summit' with the USSR's Filmmakers Union (then under the leadership of Elem Klimov, the first independently elected union leader) and several Hollywood partners, including the Writers and Directors Guilds as well as the Academy of Motion Picture Arts and Sciences. Together we analysed a century of 'anti-capitalist' films made in the USSR and 'anti-communist' films made in Hollywood. The conclusion of our 'Summit' was clear: the films made by the two superpowers of the twentieth century were a non-stop indictment of each other's governments, and an insult to each other's national character. In addition to many other political and ideological factors that contributed to the hostility of the cold war, the Russian and American people learned to fear and hate each other's leaders because they had been systematically trained from birth to do so, not only in their classrooms, but also in their cinemas.

With the end of the cold war twenty years ago, an opportunity arose for a new relationship, one based on trust, mutual interest, and collaboration. But instead of realizing this opportunity and forging a mutually beneficial alliance, old stereotypes and suspicions continue to haunt the relationship.

The consensus that emerged at a recent Russian-American dialogue was that a 'toxic cold war residue' of anachronistic attitudes was undermining the possibility of a mutually supportive, vigorous partnership between Russia and the US. In other words, leaders in both Moscow and Washington have failed to "un-learn" the cold war.[7]

As this example underscores, the learning that leads to innovative global problem-solving requires letting go of some of what we may firmly believe is 'true'. To claim our global future, we have to re-examine our culturally limited education.

● ● ● ● ● ● ● ● ● ● ● ● ● ● ●

🌐 United Nations Leadership University. Amman, Jordan. June 2003.

Invited by the United Nations University Leadership Academy (UNU/LA) to participate in a symposium on global leadership, I find myself with a group of twenty leadership scholars and practitioners from all over the world being led by an Indian trainer named Sudanshu Palsule. His capacity to work with this diverse group is so exceptional that I ask him whether I can interview him about how he developed such a remarkable skill in cross-cultural facilitation.

'When I design and conduct meetings around the world today,' he replies, 'I approach them with a certain philosophy. It is that real knowledge, *universal* knowledge, is created at the threshold, the frontiers. It emerges at the places where cultures encounter each other. Let's meet there – at the frontier!'

This philosophy grows out of the experience of his life. In order to practise his global craft, he had to unlearn much of what he was taught.

'I learned in my school to look at India through Western eyes,' explains Sudanshu, who is now an executive coach with clients from Mumbai to Atlanta. 'My education was filled with stories about English castles and London streets, Wordsworth and Chaucer, Columbus and Vasco da Gama. As a boy growing up in a recently independent India, I was still taught that India was discovered by Europeans!'

● ● ● ● ● ● ● ● ● ● ● ● ● ● ●

Being taught a partial view of the world as a child can be overcome if, repeat if, we *un*-learn what was not true. But what if we do not un-learn it? What happens if we carry these mistaken beliefs with us for the rest of our lives?

For example, one of the most difficult illusions to release is the comforting idea that our own nation is 'the greatest nation on Earth'. This notion has been so prevalent in all of the 'great powers' of the twentieth century. First London, Paris, Berlin, and then Moscow and Washington suffered from the dangerous myth that their city was the centre of the world.

'I will depart office proud of my administration's record,' said then President George W. Bush in his final radio address to the American people, only three days before Barack Obama and his family would move into the White House. 'And I will spend the rest of my life grateful for the opportunity to have served as President of *the greatest nation on Earth*.'

In the speeches of American Presidents, the phrase 'greatest nation on Earth' has been a kind of patriotic mantra for generations. It has inspired Americans to perform heroic feats and acts of great vision and generosity. As we count the number of Olympic medals won by US athletes, or measure the value of the dollar compared to other currencies, or read global opinion polls, we Americans often look for proof that we are still the greatest. Unfortunately, this illusory vanity has limited our ability to lead – and to learn.

The problem with the captivating notion that one's own country is superior to all others in every way becomes quickly apparent to even the most casual international traveller. Take a few flights around the globe and one can quickly find other countries whose leaders – and whose citizens – think they too are 'the greatest nation on Earth'.

Travelling not long ago in Jordan (which has its own streak of self-importance), I spoke with a colleague at the United Nations

Leadership Academy, Odeh Al-Jayousi, a Palestinian refugee who now teaches at the University of Jordan, who heightened my awareness of this pattern. 'I was brought up to think that the centre of the world was the Middle East, and Mecca was its capital. When I was travelling and met a Greek, he said that Athens was the centre of the world – the birthplace of Western civilization. The Jews, of course, call themselves the "chosen people" and consider Israel to have a special destiny that justifies unique rights and privileges. A colleague from South Asia told me that India was the centre of the world. Now many Americans say, "We are the centre of the world because we have the most advanced technology and the military." '

Consider a few other examples of this 'we are the greatest' syndrome:

- Journey through the People's Republic of China, and it is clear that many Chinese feel their civilization is not only the oldest, but the greatest. This national and ethnic pride lingers just beneath the communist surface, and emerges whenever there is crisis or threat.
- One of the reasons Iran is so angry, and so determined to become a nuclear power, is that many of its leaders consider it too the 'greatest nation on Earth'. The word 'Persia', so often uttered in place of the more common term Iran, is resonant with meaning for so many. This is the cradle of civilization, many Persians believe, and they refuse to be relegated to lower status.
- Listen to the tone of pronouncements from the Kremlin. Leader after leader, no matter how different in personality, continues to speak of 'mother Russia' as if it is the pre-eminent nation on Earth. After the break-up

of the Soviet Union, this pride was tarnished. But it is clear that the upper echelons in Moscow are eager to restore their country to its former greatness.

- And then there is France. Even though its empire never rivalled the British, that does not stop the French from imagining themselves to be the greatest and certainly the most refined European nation. Given the superiority of Europe for so long, that is only one step away from being 'the greatest nation on Earth'.

The truth is that China, Russia, Iran, and France have considerable company. Saudi Arabia, India, Argentina (before its own economic crash), Greece, Turkey, and of course, despite everything, Germany – these and many other nations have succumbed to the notion that they too are 'the greatest'.

This national pride is harmless, some would claim. After all, it is only natural to be proud of where one lives. If feeling superior to all other nationalities inspires a people to achieve their goals, why begrudge them this comfort? What is wrong with leaders of dozens of nations all telling their people that they are superior to everyone else?

The problem with this 'we are the greatest' belief system is that it spawns several toxic corollaries, including the following:

1. Our nation is right and never makes mistakes. (This prevents us from seeing when we are wrong, and apologizing for our errors.)
2. We have privileges or rights that citizens of other nations do not have. (This creates a double standard that other nations resent.)
3. We are naturally dominant. (This corollary leads to arrogant notions of superiority, an inability to partner, and – at it worst – oppression.)

4. International rules don't apply to us. (This leads to an isolated and unilateral foreign policy.)

The net effect of these four corollaries is that we become arrogant without even knowing it.

As global citizens, we can still value our own country and culture. But we cannot be arrogant. It is a small difference, but with enormous implications. To understand why, all we have to do is think about our friendships. If we know people who value who they are, it attracts us to them. If, however, they are arrogant about who they are, and act as if they are better than us, it repels us. By shifting from an arrogant perspective of being 'the greatest' to being a valuable part of the larger whole, we can evolve beyond Citizen 3.0 toward a more inclusive identity.

● ● ● ● ● ● ● ● ● ● ● ● ● ● ●

❂ Rose Hospital Delivery Room. Denver, Colorado. March 2008.

As I hold Isaiah, my third grandson, in my arms moments after his birth, the beauty of his face overwhelms me. I gaze at this new soul, less than fifteen minutes old, and see his resemblance to his parents.

An African-American woman with some Cherokee ancestors, his mother, Rita, is lying in the hospital bed, exhausted but radiant. My oldest son, Shane, is holding her hand, his white skin flushed pink by both the exhaustion and joy of a successful birth. My two older grandsons, with whom Shane and Rita have blessed us, have very different skin colours. Shane Jr.'s face has a Barack Obama hue, while his younger brother Luke's skin reminds me of a dark Hawaiian honey.

As Isaiah begins sucking on my finger, I hand him back to

Rita, who places him at her breast. Immediately, Isaiah begins to nurse. His eyes close and he drops into quiet bliss.

I know that I will never call him 'white' or 'black' or 'brown'. He is simply my grandson. He is Isaiah.

● ● ● ● ● ● ● ● ● ● ● ● ● ● ● ●

In 1987, a New Zealand-born biochemist, Allan Wilson, and his American colleague Rebecca Cann sent a letter to hospitals around the world asking them to send their laboratory a placenta. After studying the genetic material in the cells of a hundred and forty-seven samples (called the 'mitochondrial DNA'), they concluded that all were traceable to a common ancestor. They hypothesized that all of humanity was the offspring of this common ancestor, who before long was referred to as the 'African Eve'. She gave birth to the first modern humans, who began spreading around the world about fifty to a hundred thousand years ago.

Twenty years of research only refined the analysis further. The origin of all human life – the 'Garden of Eden', some called it rather ethnocentrically – was in south-west Africa. The rest of the world was populated, according to precise DNA data, by a relatively small band of Africans who left that continent via the African coast on the Red Sea.[8]

The hypothesis was controversial – a 'bombshell', in the words of Nayan Chanda, an Indian journalist who has closely researched the subject. If correct, it meant that *every human being is a relative of all the others*. This was the anthropological equivalent of orbiting around the Earth. After all, if one believed this hypothesis, the so-called divisions of humankind – separating Muslim from Christian or Jew, Caucasian from African or Asian – were genetic illusions. No matter what one's ethnic identity, everyone was tied to everyone else. We were all, literally, distant cousins.

Among many others, the Chinese were not pleased by the genetic information that indicated that their great civilization had begun in Africa. The notion that their original ancestors were 'African', genetically speaking, did not appeal to their national pride. They knew about the so-called 'Peking man', also called *Sinanthropus pekinensis* (or *Homo erectus pekinensis*), whose remains were discovered in 1923–27 during excavations at Zhoukoudian near Beijing. They believed that the Chinese had their own lineage, and that they were the most ancient civilization on Earth. Specifically, their traditional explanation was that they were all descendants of the Yellow Emperor, who established his kingdom in the area now called China. So for many Chinese, the concept of an 'African Eve' challenged many of their cultural and historical truths.

Chinese geneticist Li Jin and his students decided to put the hypothesis to the test. They collected DNA samples from ten thousand Chinese males. Every single one of them fitted the prototype found by Wilson, Cann, and their colleagues.

'We looked,' Jin concluded in 2000. 'Modern humans originated in Africa.'[9]

Following the same rigorous methods, geneticists have replicated the findings. Not only have they confirmed that we all descend from the same genetic source, but they can trace the direction and timing of our ancestors journey across the face of the Earth. Our bodies, our faces, our language, and of course skin pigmentation have become diverse. But that, scientists tell us, is the only surface. Underneath the differences, we are all one.

A common response to this scientific breakthrough, even today, is denial. Faced with the obvious reality that some human beings are black as coal, while others are white as snow, we find it hard, if not impossible, to believe that 'we are all one'.

If, repeat *if*, we are willing to unlearn our ideas about race, science can explain the spectrum of skin colours that form humanity's palette. Lighter skin enables the absorption of more sun, which is what catalyses vitamin D in the human body and enables calcium intake. In the north, where there was far less sunshine, natural selection favoured those with lighter skins. (Because mothers need more vitamin D to bear and nurse children, some believe this is why their skin is 3–4 per cent lighter than men's in every population.)[10]

The genetic evidence establishing humanity's oneness is as revolutionary as the first photos of the Earth from outer space. It is a true discovery, precisely because it challenges our preconceptions. 'There is no race,' says Luis Quintana-Murci of the Pasteur Institute in Paris, only 'geographic gradients.' We invent the hard lines that divide us into races; they do not, in fact, exist.[11]

If we want personal evidence that we, too, are part of this shared hereditary history, we can pay a fee and trace our DNA. This is precisely what Frances Drabick did, and it profoundly changed her view of herself and the world overnight. A resident of Eastport, Maine, a small town in the north-east corner of the USA, she previously described herself as Polish-American because her parents came from Poland; they spoke Polish; and they celebrated Polish traditions. But when she had her DNA tested, the results were startling.

Her father's genetic legacy, according to the DNA tests, revealed that her lineage included Palestinians, Jordanians, Greeks, Turks, Iranians, Arabs and Jews (Israel), and Uzbeks (Chinese Turkestan). Add various Scottish genetic strands from her mother's side of the family, and Frances Drabick finally had a portrait of her genetic heritage.

'Now I know more than I could have imagined,' Drabick says. 'The revelations have opened not only my mind but also my heart, to the struggles of so many good people who I now know are my closest genetic relatives.' However, she wonders: 'Can we open our hearts and minds without the use of genetic tests?'[12]

Even without a DNA test, global citizens can study their own family tree through research and imagination. We can genetically link ourselves to one of the branches of humanity's hundred-thousand-year migration and find out exactly who our ancestors were and where their walk began. But if we do so, *we must be prepared to change our attitudes about race*. Whether our skin is black or white, whether our nose is thin like most northern Europeans or broad like most Ethiopians, whether our body is short and thick like the Samoans or tall and slender like many Finns, we will obtain scientific data that we are part of the whole that is called humankind.

It is a discovery that embodies all the challenges and rewards of cross-boundary learning because it requires the courage to risk discovering something that makes us question who we are – and how we see this world. To become global citizens, we cannot stop learning at every wall that is erected, every boundary that is created. We cannot accept one story as 'the truth' when in fact we need to listen to many.

● ● ● ● ● ● ● ● ● ● ● ● ● ● ● ●

🌐 **Firdos Square, Baghdad. 9 April 2003.**

Like millions of others around the world, I am watching television (in my case, CNN). As American troops seize control of the capital city of Iraq, demonstrations break out among the Iraqi people. Citizens converge at a square in downtown Baghdad where a huge statue of Saddam Hussein is cemented into a heavy pedestal. First, Iraqis try using ordinary tools, including an axe, to knock it over. But it soon becomes clear that more power is required.

Then someone attaches a strong cable to a vehicle (which is off-screen). Finally, the statue topples.

As soon as it falls, a throng of demonstrators begin jumping on it, pounding it with their shoes and hitting it with their fists. Some commentators compare the moment when Germans tore down the Berlin Wall, or Hungarians knocked down statues of Stalin and other icons of Soviet communism.

• • • • • • • • • • • • • • • •

Search for a YouTube video using the words 'Firdos Square Saddam statue' and you can watch this scene yourself. But what appears on the screen is data, or information; the key is in its interpretation. For many in Europe and the US, the interpretation of the scene at Firdos Square was self-evident. We interpreted the scene based on the narrative already in our minds: namely, that the Iraqi people were celebrating the fall of a dictator who had held them in a grip of terror for a generation and were spontaneously expressing their suppressed rage and jubilation.

According to a US Army report, however, this interpretation is flawed. Based on this report, the statue was not pulled down by Iraqis at all. The chain that dislodged the twenty-foot-high bronze statue was connected to a US Marine recovery vehicle. In fact, as described by the official military report, the statue was torn down under direct orders from an army colonel in the 'psychological operations' (PSYOPS) unit who recognized the setting as a 'target of opportunity'. He provided a Marine recovery vehicle with a long chain in order to topple the statue, thereby creating a photo opportunity showing 'ordinary citizens' celebrating the fall of the dictator.

To turn the scene into effective political propaganda, the scene required a cast of 'spontaneous' citizens demonstrating their hatred for the dictator. Wide-angle shots of Firdos Square – which were never shown on American television – show the entire area carefully cordoned off by American tanks. These photographs and videos show a vacant Firdos Square, and then a truck arriving transporting the 'demonstrators' who will, moments later, be angrily stamping on the statue. Based on these wide-angle shots, the scene is not a spontaneous citizen uprising, but a staging area controlled and scripted by PSYOPS. According to this interpretation, although the demonstrators were anti-Saddam activists who were genuinely expressing their rage, they had been strategically selected and transported by the US military to the site for the purpose of creating the desired 'photo opportunity'.

As any student of filmmaking could have predicted, however, the 'shoot' was more complicated than the military directors anticipated. In an unscripted moment, an enthusiastic marine, Corporal Edward Chin from New York of the 3rd Battalion, 4th Marines regiment, climbed up the statue and draped an American flag over Saddam Hussein's face. Suddenly, the energy in the Iraqi crowd faded because they, of course, wanted to see their own flag. The PSYOPS officers immediately knew they had made a serious blunder.

'This was just bad news,' one member of the PSYOPS unit said. 'We didn't want to look like an occupation force, and some of the Iraqis were saying, "No, we want an Iraqi flag!" When the Stars and Stripes were finally replaced, the man who put the Iraqi flag in its place was not a courageous Iraqi freedom fighter. It was a sergeant in the PSYOPS unit.'[13]

But the damage had already been done. The effort to create a scene of jubilant Iraqi citizens reclaiming their country from a dictator had been undermined by a zealous marine caught in an Iwo Jima time-warp. Instead of making it appear that the Iraqis were reclaiming their own country, his patriotic impulse inadvertently drew attention to the fact that the statue was being torn down by a foreign army, not the people themselves.

Despite the controlled access to the square, unauthorized observers provided independent accounts of what happened that day. 'The crowd is still milling around Firdos Square, but they have stopped trying to topple Saddam's monument,' observed Fred Kaplan in a Web posting on that very day. 'And now, here comes the American tank. The Iraqis are now tying a steel chain, no doubt U.S.-supplied, to the statue, and the Abrams M1 will serve as the toppler.'

'Oh, no; it's getting worse,' Kaplan continued. 'Marines are getting up on the statue to pull it down themselves. One of them has draped an American flag over Saddam's head. *What a moron!* It's the very picture of neo-colonialism, which will make front pages all over the Arab world. Now he's taking off the American flag. No doubt, someone from Centcom, watching CNN, phoned the officer on the scene to chew him out and remind him of the orders against such displays.'[14]

As global citizens, we cannot read or watch the news without learning how to integrate disparate, and often conflicting, narratives. Like so many other historical moments captured by the media, the toppling of Saddam's statue in Firdos Square is not *a* story. It is *many* stories. The challenge facing us as global citizens is to decode these stories and consciously construct our own point of view. Which story, then, do *you* believe? Do you believe Story 1: a spontaneous Iraqi demonstration? Story 2: an Iraqi demonstration enhanced with the technical assistance of an American tank? Or Story 3: a scene totally manufactured by the US Army PSYOPS unit designed to manipulate the media into vindicating the US-led invasion?

For Citizens 1.0–3.0, these multiple versions are intolerable. They want to believe that their group, or their country, is right and others, therefore, must be wrong. But as we evolve into Citizen 4.0–5.0, we recognize the likelihood of encountering multiple versions of reality and we accept that it is our responsibility to learn to make sense out of them

Whatever your point of view, we can use the multiple stories about the events on 9 April 2003 at Firdos Square – and other controversial global events – as opportunities to learn beyond borders. With absolute certainty, we can anticipate that the challenge of decoding competing versions of the same event will emerge again and again. It is an inevitable part of living in a global village.[15]

• • • • • • • • • • • • • • •

Davos, Switzerland, and Porto Alegre, Brazil. January 2001.

'You are our enemies,' the woman in a white shawl said angrily. Looking directly at the face of the billionaire George Soros on the video screen in front of her, she shouted: 'How many children are killed each day because of your plans?'

The woman in the shawl, Señora de Bonafini, is one of the Mothers of the Plaza de Mayo, an organization of Argentinean women who lost loved ones at the hands of the military. Sitting in Porto Alegre, Brazil, attending the World Social Forum (WSF) in January 2001, she was shouting at four white men in suits, including Soros, whose images were flickering on a video screen connected by satellite to Davos, Switzerland, the site of the World Economic Forum (WEF).

The four men, who include two businessmen and two UN officials, agreed to participate in the videobridge linking these two events, which are often referred to simply as 'Davos' or 'Porto Alegre' after the cities in which they typically convene. Because WSF was founded in opposition to WEF – to 'put it out of business', as one of the radical Brazilian participants put it – the air was filled with tension. And it fell to this grey-haired woman to put the unspoken feelings into words.

'Tell us,' shouted the Argentinean activist even more loudly, 'how many more deaths can we expect from capitalism or globalization or whatever you call it? Tell us, gentlemen! You're like monsters, eating everything up. You are eating us up! As a mother, I ask you, how many children are you killing each day?'

Then Señora de Bonafini saw a tight, nervous smile appear on the face of George Soros, a multimillionaire financial speculator and philanthropist who regularly attends the Davos meeting. He is perhaps best known for his skilful investing in (or, according to his critics, 'plundering' or 'prof-iteering from') fluctuating currencies. Enraged, Señora de Bonafini unexpectedly turned her general attack on capitalism into a personal attack on him.

'Mr Soros with his face of a hypocrite, smiling at the deaths of millions of children from hunger!' she screamed at the screen. 'Look at me, Mr Soros, look at my face if you dare!'

'I am looking at your face and I'm smiling because that's

the only thing I can do,' replied Mr Soros quietly, obviously shaken by this unexpected personal attack bouncing through space across the Atlantic Ocean. 'I am trying to have a dialogue with you, but you don't seem to want to have a dialogue with me. So we might as well stop talking.'

And then, sadly, he leaned back in his chair and fell silent.

• • • • • • • • • • • • • •

At a cost of over one hundred thousand dollars, this well-intentioned videobridge had harnessed cutting-edge satellite technology to link these two polarized events. This brief, ninety-minute window for face-to-face communication was the only opportunity for the wealthy and powerful Davos participants to transcend the boundaries of their well-guarded Swiss ski village, which was surrounded by security forces keeping anti-globalization demonstrators at bay. It was also the only opportunity the representatives of the impoverished majority of the world had to break through the cordon of Swiss police and talk with the men and women to whom they often refer as the 'corporate elite'.

For many years two of the most influential non-governmental gatherings in the world today, the wealthy, predominantly corporate-oriented leaders in Switzerland and the tens of thousands of NGOs and grassroots groups gathered in Porto Alegre, represented a polarized microcosm of 'global citizenship' in the world today. Observing what happens when the two 'sides' encountered each other provides a revealing lens through which to view the way in which 'global leaders' speak to each other.

Unfortunately, the WEF and WSF representatives – who included some of the most caring, committed, and knowledge-

able diplomats, entrepreneurs, and activists of our time –
were casualties of a communication pattern that is as
common as it is inefficient. Instead of forging an ascending
path to the high ground of trust-building dialogue, they chose
instead the all too common, descending road of mistrustful
debate. It was a wrong turn, and it led to a dead end. Learning
was not catalysed; it was killed.

On a personal level, learning is optional. Every citizen is free to
decide when, or if, he or she wishes to learn. But if we want to
evolve toward becoming global citizens, then cross-boundary
learning is no longer optional. It becomes a matter of moral as
well as intellectual necessity because global problem-solving
requires building bridges between groups that are divided by
cultural, economic, and ideological identities. Global citizens are
committed to listen and to learn – even if it means discovering
that we may be wrong.

If the participants had wanted to make their videobridge a
true cross-boundary learning experience, they would have
defined their encounter as a dialogue to witness and learn rather
than as a debate to 'win'. Despite common misperceptions to the
contrary, 'dialogue' does not mean that they are willing to soften
their views, or to abandon other more militant, polarizing
strategies. But it does mean that they are willing to question their
assumptions and be open to truths other than their own.

After a year of false starts and dead ends, my colleagues and
I invited representatives of both the World Economic Forum
and the World Social Forum to join us at a meeting entitled the
'Bridge Initiative on Globalization'. The eight representatives of
both 'Davos' and 'Porto Alegre' (who will remain anonymous, as

we agreed) were joined, at their request, by seven high-level representatives of the major global governance institutions: the International Monetary Fund (IMF), the World Bank, and the World Trade Organization (WTO).

As they eyed each other suspiciously around the circle, their initial comments revealed their wariness and their sense of hope. When we asked them at the beginning of the meeting what would make it a 'success' in their eyes, their responses were illuminating.

'I don't have all the answers,' said one of the corporate executives who were part of the WEF delegation. 'Finding them will require *all* of us.'

'Is it possible to move from debate to dialogue – or at least to a more direct and honest debate?' asked one of the multilateral organization officials.

'Let's admit it,' said one of the participants from Porto Alegre. 'None of us knows how to develop a coherent alternative to the current system, which is dysfunctional and unjust.'

Over an agonizing but ultimately catalytic thirty-six hours, this unprecedented mixture of global voices shifted from wariness to wondering, from mistrust to hope. By creating a trust-building environment which honoured listening rather than speechmaking, the energy shifted. So when we asked each participant at the end of the gathering what they had learned, their replies were heartfelt.

'We have moved from deliberate image-building to developing a more neutral space,' said one participant. 'My recommendation to my director-general will be that we come with an open mind to future meetings – as long as it continues to be neutral . . . that is my only condition.'

'Both our disagreement and agreements here have been

useful,' said his counterpart from Porto Alegre. 'This closed informal meeting should lead to a larger public forum.'

'I leave with the hope that we have begun to break down the confrontation,' said one of the intergovernmental organization representatives.

Said another senior Davos delegate: 'I believe we have proven that we are capable of transcending established positions in order to move forward together.'

'After twenty years working in this field, this is the first significant meeting where process has been the focus instead of policy,' said a veteran official of the IMF. 'I wish this had happened twenty years ago.'

As a delegate from Porto Alegre summed up: 'We have taken the first step toward building a bridge.'

Why were the results of this meeting so different than the videobridge? They were different because of the methods we used. Instead of bringing them in front of separate cameras to film their conflict, we brought them physically together to begin learning together how to solve the specific global problems about which both organizations care deeply. As I explain in detail in my previous book, Leading Through Conflict, if we skilfully use the basic tools of conflict transformation, we can turn even the deepest differences into opportunities for learning and then shared action.[16]

Again and again, when groups convene that represent the full range of views on an issue or the whole system, I observe this inspiring transformation from arrogance to humility. *Whenever diverse groups of people focus with opens minds and hearts on the complex challenges facing humanity, a remarkable alchemy often occurs. First, pride subsides. Then humility emerges. And, finally, if we are fortunate, we begin to learn from each other.*

No matter how great our differences, no matter how deep the tensions between diverse factions and groups, a common purpose emerges in our midst. Those who know the most are often the quietest, and those who know the least are often the quickest to speak. This is because learning about the Earth and all the life it sustains inspires humility (from the root *humus*, meaning 'earth' or 'ground'.) One cannot strive over many years to know, and to love, this Earth without admitting that one is not an expert at all, but a grateful student of our common home.

Perhaps humility is the ultimate lesson of cross-boundary learning. Instead of becoming more arrogant – with our visual 'superpowers' that enable us to see everywhere, and our telecommunication 'superpowers' that empower us to speak to anyone anywhere, and our military 'superpowers' that allow us to kill anyone anywhere – we become more humble. Instead of puffing out our chests with pride about how much we do know, we bow our heads in reverence to what we do not.

● ● ● ● ● ● ● ● ● ● ● ● ● ●

🌐 Tehran, Iran. November 2002.

In a lecture at a leading university, history professor Hashem Aghajari argued that in order for Islam to remain a living religion, each new generation must be entitled to interpret Islam for itself. He maintained that followers of Mohammed should not be expected to adopt existing interpretations as the final truth but can and must think independently for themselves.

Outraged, fundamentalist Islamic clerics, who dominate the Iranian judiciary, claimed that he had insulted the Prophet Mohammed and sentenced him to death. Huge demonstrations erupted at major universities defending him.

'If his comments deserve death,' says one student demonstrator, 'then kill us all.' Even the Iranian President,
Mohammad Khatami, who sought progressive reform, stated
publicly that such a sentence 'never should have been issued
at all'.

● ● ● ● ● ● ● ● ● ● ● ● ● ● ●

All of our tribal, religious/racial, national, and ideological
boundaries exist because we human beings have created them.
Cross-boundary learning is about 'deconstructing' the boundaries
so that we, like the astronauts, can see the essential unity of the
whole.

Using this 'internal passport', we do not have to stop at the
borders our cultures have created for us. We can cross the
border that separates Catholic from Protestant, Sunni from Shi'ite,
corporate executive from anti-corporate critic, Tribe A from Tribe
B, and Party X from Party Y. Because these borders were created
by human beings, they can be crossed by us as well. By transcending unnecessary borders, we free ourselves. We can still
cherish our own faith, respect our own country, and honour our
own tribe, lineage or clan. But as global citizens, our roots
nourish us, but will not confine us. *Our minds and hearts will be
free to travel anywhere, anytime.*

To cross boundaries with this internal passport, however,
requires a capacity to learn and witness that takes us beyond pre-
fabricated ideologies. An ideology is an all-purpose, ready-made
worldview (often ending in '-ism') that enables us to project our
values on any event and interpret it in ways that are self-reinforc-
ing. Our beliefs, if they change at all, will only grow more rigid.
Sealed off from the risk of learning, we are vaccinated against
doubt or questioning. The motto of Citizen 1.0–3.0 is: 'Since I

already know "the truth", I will fit everything inside it.'

By contrast, the motto of Citizen 4.0–5.0 is: 'I will witness the world as fully as I can in order to learn its deepest truths.' Global citizens consciously seek out experiences that will challenge their pre-existing views. Instead of rigidly attaching themselves to a worldview and shutting down enquiry, they remain open to new information and to the possibility of change. Their internal passport enables them to widen their identities, continually upgrading their citizenship software throughout their lives. This process of evolving as citizens is a never-ending journey of transcending and including all previous levels of identification so that, in Gandhi's words, 'we learn to identify with all that lives'.[17]

We do not 'leave behind' these earlier and narrower identities as we become global citizens. They remain a part of us, but are integrated into an ever-widening identity. As long as we are in a body, the egocentric worldview is part of who we are. Similarly, we take the other aspects of our historical selves (ideology, religion, nationality, etc.) with us. We actually need these borders to describe and organize the world. Just as a business enterprise naturally assigns certain job definitions to its employees and breaks itself up into departments or divisions, so it is understandable that we have broken the world into nations and humanity into various subgroups. But at the same time, just like a business has to operate as a whole enterprise to be effective, so do we – and the Earth – need to become aware of our oneness.

Once again, Gandhi captures the essence of this process. In his commentary on the *Bhagavad Gita*, the ancient Indian scriptures entitled 'Song of God', Gandhi teaches us a fundamental lesson about learning. Although he was so utterly committed to freeing India from British colonial rule that he dedicated his life to that cause, Gandhi made clear that he was not identified with or attached to that goal.

'Attachment to good work, is that wrong?' he asks pointedly.

'Yes, it is,' he replies. 'If we are attached to our goal of winning liberty, we shall not hesitate to adopt bad means.'[18]

As the Indian mystic Satchidananda says: 'Read the Bible, read the Koran, read the Torah, the Upanishads, the *Bhagavad Gita* . . . Get out of these definitions. It's the definitions that divide us.'[19]

● ● ● ● ● ● ● ● ● ● ● ● ● ●

🌐 Philosopher's Home. Boulder, Colorado. 1997.

Amidst a group of white male American intellectuals fascinated by the work of the philosopher and author Ken Wilber, Maureen Silos stands out immediately. A beautiful African-Caribbean woman, from the nation of Surinam (formerly Dutch Guiana), Maureen speaks with a Caribbean accent tinged by Dutch. As she shares her background, I mention that my parents were both from the Netherlands.

'Wonderful!' she tells me. 'I went to university there . . . studying with the colonizers of my people.'

She smiles warmly. But in her eyes, I see ferocity.

After a long conversation, I ask her if she would be interested in co-lecturing with me in a few months at a leadership conference in Miami for educators from all over North America and the Caribbean. I am delighted when she agrees because now, for the first time, the child of the colonizer and the colonized will be speaking *together* about leadership.

● ● ● ● ● ● ● ● ● ● ● ● ● ●

Even though her ancestors were African and Indian – from the subcontinent of India, not the indigenous 'Indians' so misnamed by the European explorers – Maureen Silos was educated in a white European system that deeply influenced her worldview. Growing up, Silos asked herself questions such as: 'Why do I speak Dutch, a language of a tiny country far across the ocean? Why are so many of my neighbours "Hindustani", with the features and traditions common halfway around the world?' As she educated herself, the answers to her questions took her back to a history that was built on the premise that the European 'master' knew what was best for his 'subjects'.

Now armed with degrees from Dutch and American universities, fluent in the languages of both the colonized and the colonizer, Maureen knows the planetary story of conquest from the inside out. It is in the marrow of her bones. She has had to reclaim her vision by freeing herself from the 'blinded eye' which sees this history as a story of progress in which all that is dark and heathen and primitive is rescued by all that is white and Christian and modern. This is why her mission is to find an alternative model of learning-based leadership, one in which all the various hyphenated parts of her being can be developed and, indeed, cherished.

'Look at me,' Silos said a few months later to the audience of mostly North American educators in Miami, as she playfully flipped the ends of her long dreadlocks into the air. 'Look at my black hair and black skin. You think I am a black Third World woman, don't you?'

Her audience nodded.

'But in fact, until recently, I was not,' she said with deliberate drama. 'I was schooled by my colonial masters. They taught me how to think. They taught me what to read. They taught me to speak their language. So *inside* I was neither African nor Caribbean; *inside*, I was European. *Inside*, I was a Western intellectual. My identity revolved around the ideas and words and theories and logic of Europe and North America. When I realized this, I was so shocked that I looked in the mirror and said to myself, *"Girl, you're white."* '

Maureen explained to her attentive audience how she finally began to reclaim the parts of herself she had forfeited to 'succeed'. She told them how, as a visiting lecturer in African-American Studies at UCLA, she delved more deeply into the split inside her, this strange half-North/half-South, half-establishment/half-revolutionary identity that had developed during her twenties and thirties. But then, just as she was completing her autobiographical overview, an American educator from North Carolina raised her hand.

'So how do you feel about America?' the woman asked pointedly. 'What do you think of the people who destroyed the World Trade Centre?'

Even though the questioner didn't put it into words, the audience could hear it in her voice. She was tired of all the complexities, impatient with all of Maureen's hyphens, suspicious of all the multicultural ambiguity. Although she dared not say it this bluntly, she was in effect asking Maureen: *Whose side are you on?*

'Thank you for asking that,' Silos replied without a trace of defensiveness. 'It will help me make my point more clearly.' After taking several steps toward the questioner, so she could look her directly in the eyes, Maureen explained that she both admired and resented America: admired the USA for its individual freedoms and entrepreneurial spirit, and resented American leaders for their arrogance.

With her voice rising in defiance, her Dutch accent almost

washed away by her passion, Maureen made it clear to her American questioner that she would not allow herself to be so easily boxed in and labelled. Despite the North Carolinian's yearning to know whether Maureen Silos was pro- or anti-American, Silos would not comply. Having worked hard for many years to become a cross-boundary learner, she was not going to fit herself into one of the convenient boundaries of her questioner. She had worked hard to become a global citizen. She was not about to stop now.

Like Maureen Silos, many citizens around the world are evolving toward Citizen 5.0. Researchers have developed psychometric tools for assessing 'global mindset', 'cross-cultural intelligence', and other concepts signifying what in the concluding chapter we will call more generally 'global intelligence'. These capacities are within each of us, but only some of us decide to develop them more fully.

Cross-boundary learning is what transforms a global mindset from an ideal into a reality. It is the foundation that makes global decision-making possible. It is based on the accurate assumption that most people grow up in what Professor Mansour Javidan calls a 'uni-cultural' context. In other words, most of us grow up with people who are like us. But now, in a globalized world, we find ourselves living and working with people who are not like us.

This is the key reason why the concepts of *global* citizenship and leadership have emerged in corporations with such compelling force. The success of business leaders now depends on integrating their activities with hundreds, sometimes thousands, of others whom (in Javidan's words) 'they may never have seen, never met, and *with whom they may not share a culture or a native language*. They have to do this extremely well – or lose their competitive global edge.'

Imagine, for example, that we are executives at Boeing or Airbus, and we are caught in a highly charged, time-sensitive competition for a multi-billion-dollar contract. Our success depends on the degree to which we can coordinate thousands of men and women who are designing and building the systems for a new aircraft. The slightest cross-cultural misunderstandings, the most minute misinterpretation of data, can – and do – lead to delays that will lose our company the contract. Seen from this perspective, global leadership is not a theoretical concept. It is a business necessity.

'We have talked to more than thirty multinational companies from all over the world,' Javidan told me passionately. 'We have not heard any other reaction to the concept of the global mindset than, "Oh my God, this is exactly what we need." '

A generation younger than Javidan, Maximilian Johnson is in total agreement. After holding jobs in finance in London and Moscow, and armed with a degree from Oxford University, Johnson was well positioned for a promising business career. He could have chosen from a variety of exciting professional opportunities in Europe or North America. But instead, he decided to study for his master's degree in the People's Republic of China.

'As companies look to expand in emerging markets,' Johnson explained, 'they will need MBAs who have both the business knowledge and the ability to navigate multicultural situations. This is the advantage of an MBA from a business school in China.'[20]

Executive recruiters at leading firms such as Korn/Ferry International report that corporate boards are now very clear that they want CEOs with multi-cultural experience. They are either hiring leaders from outside their own country of origin, or are looking for domestic talent that has spent at least part of their careers in different countries.

- Susan Bishop, a spokeswoman for General Electric: 'As you move through the company and you're looked at for a promotion, one of the things we are going to look at is, do you have international experience?'
- Marijn E. Dekkers, the Dutch CEO of an American high-tech company, Thermo Fisher Scientific: 'You're not intimidated doing business with people who are different than you. I'm more open to exploring doing business in Asia, even though I'm from Europe.'
- Farooq Kathwari, CEO of Ethan Allen Furniture, based in New England: 'A foreign-born person is by nature an entrepreneur. When you leave your home, leave your family and come to a different country, you have had the instincts of an entrepreneur.'[21]
- Top high-tech executive at a recent Beijing conference: 'Chinese companies are growing so rapidly that we need leaders who know how to deal with non-Chinese. The era of the China-only executive is over.'[22]
- Anil Gupta, Vijay Govindarajan and Haiyan Wang, three Asian specialists on global business: 'Global managers don't passively accept it when someone says, "You can't do that in Italy or Spain because of the unions," or, "You can't do that in Japan because of the Ministry of Finance." They sort through the debris of cultural excuses and find opportunities to innovate.'[23]
- Michael Useem, a management professor at the Wharton School at the University of Pennsylvania: 'Even though they're based in the United States, companies are less and less thinking of themselves as American companies.'[24]

As all these voices attest, the global bottom line is that a company can succeed across borders only to the degree that it is able to witness and learn about the rapidly changing world in which it must compete.

● ● ● ● ● ● ● ● ● ● ● ● ● ● ●

🌐 Integrated Research Corporate Offices. North Sydney, Australia.

'Why is an entrepreneur who founded a high-tech company getting involved with the issue of war and peace?' I asked Steve Killelea, Chairman and founder of Integrated Research Ltd.

It is a question I have wanted to ask him ever since I encountered the Global Peace Index, which ranks all the nations of the world in terms of the degree to which they are violence-free. I was truly curious about how a businessman who has developed two highly profitable global companies with customers in over fifty countries had decided to create a not-for-profit peace organization.

'I have a private foundation that I set up about ten years ago and it has taken me to many of the poorest countries in the world. About three years ago I was in Africa wandering through some of the most disastrous war zones, and I asked myself: "What does the opposite look like, who are the most peaceful nations and what can we learn from them that could be used to make these places more peaceful?" I was amazed when I realized that there was no list of the most peaceful nations in the world so I decided to develop the Global Peace Index.'

The question made Steve realize how little we actually understand about peace. As he began to search for the answer to his question, he only became more curious. He went to the major universities of the world and he couldn't find a single course on the economics of peace. (There were no courses either about the literature of peace or the history of peace.) So Steve began to design his own course on peace based around the GPI, and in the end concluded that the major challenges facing humanity in the twenty-first century revolve around the sustainability of the planet such as climate change, ever-decreasing bio-diversity, full use of fresh water, and, underpinning all of this, over-population.

'Without a world that is basically peaceful, then we will never get the levels of cooperation, inclusiveness, or social equity necessary to solve the problems let alone empower the international institutions to create the governances necessary and to implement the policies; therefore, peace is the prerequisite for the survival of civilization as we know it. Today, peace is in everyone's self-interest.'

When I returned to my hotel room, I put 'global peace index' into my search engine and looked up my country, the United States of America. It ranked 97 out of 140 countries. And I wished that every person in the world, no matter where they lived, would be as eager to learn their country's ranking on the GPI as they were about their GNP.

● ● ● ● ● ● ● ● ● ● ● ● ● ● ● ●

Since corporate leaders now understand the imperative of thinking globally, the focus of business education has shifted accordingly. The phrase that is ricocheting through the universities of the world is Global Workforce Development (GWD). The term GWD, says Ron Moffatt, the late director of the San Diego State University International Student Center, 'has come to mean a global-ready graduate, that is, a person with a grasp of global systems, global issues, the dynamics of how things are inter-related and interconnected in the world.' [25]

Whether it is the University of Chicago Business School in Singapore or INSEAD in Paris or the Wharton School in Philadelphia, those who provide master's degrees in business administration are gravitating to curricula that emphasize cross-boundary learning. They are creating student bodies that are global; seeking professors who are global; creating teaching materials that are global; and promoting career paths that are global. This is not a temporary trend or current fad; it is a deep, long-term, and sustained shift in the way we approach management education. Business students are learning about the fundamental interconnectedness of business life.

Consequently, countries around the world are now vying for the international student market. The global competition for students is 'heating up', writes Daniel Obst of the Institute of International Education. Many nations are trying to position themselves as the best source for a global education. Although its market share is dropping, the USA still attracts the largest number of 'internationally mobile' students (22 per cent), with the UK, Germany, France, and Australia following in that order.[26]

The scramble for executives who are global citizens is a direct result of economic pressures on today's multinational corpora-tions – or what IBM CEO Sam Palmisano more accurately calls the 'global integrated enterprise'. According to Palmisano: 'Hierarchical command-and-control approaches simply do not work anymore. They impede information flows inside companies, hampering the fluid and collaborative nature of work today.' Because of the challenge of 'maintain[ing] trust in enterprises based on increasingly distributed business models,' he says, new kinds of executive skills are need. 'A reliance on hierarchies contained within one function, enterprise or nation must be supplemented by new ways of establishing trust, based on *shared values that cross borders* . . . '[27]

The global, high-tech, knowledge economy is forcing multi-national corporations to learn beyond borders to a degree never before imagined. To succeed, they must 'build a new kind of competitive advantage by discovering, accessing, mobilizing and leveraging knowledge from many locations around the world.'[28] Unlike the old multinationals, which Yves Doz, a distinguished professor of global technology and innovation based in France and Singapore, predicts will 'run into increasing social tensions and increasing political strife', the more decentralized and agile 'metanationals' will not be dominated by their home base. They will instead 'innovate *by learning from the world.*'[29]

What is true for the companies themselves is even truer for those who are employed by them. 'The cornerstone of a prosperous nation is its intellectual capital,' observes Dilip Murkerjea, a Singapore-based business consultant. 'Brain-power has replaced horsepower.' In this 'Age of Competitive Intelligence', Murkerjea believes that the way we harness human intelligence 'is the only source of strategic competitive advantage.' For this reason, he says: 'The manager of the future will be a learning guide.'[30]

This focus on cross-boundary learning is not only emerging in global crossroads like Singapore, but also in hard-core industrial enterprises in traditional sectors of the economy. 'In your career, knowledge is like milk,' observes former Ford Motor Company's chief technology officer, Louis Ross. 'It has a shelf life stamped right on the carton.' Estimating that a degree in engineering has a 'shelf life' of approximately three years, Ross concludes: 'If you're not replacing everything you know by then, your career is going to turn sour fast.'[31]

Trying to cope with the breakneck speed of change in a cyber-driven global economy, organizations and nations that play by the old rules are falling behind. The new rules of learning organizations – moving beyond blame, avoiding symptomatic solutions, focusing on areas of high leverage, thinking systemically – are not a passing trend, but a fact of life.[32]

At her desk at *The Economist*, Frances Cairncross has observed the shrinking of the world, or what she calls the 'death of distance'. She concludes: 'In a world where, for the vast majority, information flows freely, the penalties for restricting it will be impoverishment and marginalization.' Even in those parts of the world where computers are scarce and cyberspace inaccessible, leadership based on walls is crumbling too.[33]

We need boundary-crossing learners because the old local and national 'know-it-alls' cannot deal with today's world. Whether we are military officers or executives, teachers or farmers, professors or students, only cross-boundary learning will provide us with the internal passport that we need to navigate throughout our interconnected world.

Chapter 3

Connecting:
Creating Relationships

We are technologically closer – and culturally and politically as far apart as ever. Maybe the Internet, fiber optics, and satellites really are, together, like a high-tech Tower of Babel. It's as though God suddenly gave us all the tools to communicate and none of the tools to understand.

— Thomas Friedman, American journalist

Love is the only emotion that enhances our intelligence.

— Humberto Maturana, Chilean biologist

Blindfolded, his arms tightly gripped by his two armed captors, the UN diplomat Giandomenico Picco was brought into a room where the leader of the kidnappers was waiting to interrogate him.

Picco found himself in a terrorist hideout in Beirut in 1991 because the Secretary-General of the United Nations had asked him to negotiate the release of hostages. Nevertheless, despite his official status, he was terrified. Even though he had agreed in advance to be picked up in the middle of the night by these Muslim extremists, he now wondered whether the whole idea was a big mistake.

When Picco's blindfold was finally removed, he was facing a well-built, black-haired Arab man in his late thirties wearing a ski mask. Behind the narrow slits in the ski mask, Picco could see nothing except the dark, suspicious eyes of his captor.

'You may know something about me,' Giandomenico Picco said, after a period of silence. 'But I know nothing about you.'

'What do you want to know?' the masked leader asked Picco.

Picco paused before he spoke again. He knew the words he chose would determine the hostages' fate – and perhaps his own.

Imagine, just for a moment, that you are this Italian envoy of the United Nations sent to a Middle Eastern country to secure the release of hostages being held by 'militants'. You have been picked up in a car, guarded by four men with machine guns. You are blindfolded, and taken to an undisclosed location. You are utterly alone and defenceless. None of your UN colleagues knows the location where you are being held. When your blindfold is removed, you are surrounded by masked men armed with machine guns. Completely at the mercy of your captors, you wonder whether you will survive the night. You think of your loved ones, and are afraid that you may never see them again.

The challenge that Picco faced was not mere 'communication'. If it were, that would be the title of this chapter. But to communicate – 'the exchange of information between individuals by means of speaking, writing, or using a common system of signs or behaviour' – is relatively easy. The ultimate challenge facing Picco, and any global citizen, is not merely to communicate, but to *connect*. The challenge of connecting is to build a bridge of trust across a divide in order that the two or more individuals or groups can work together more effectively.

For most of us, fortunately, the stakes are not as high as they were for this UN official. But precisely because the circumstances facing Picco were extreme, his situation crystallizes the challenge of connecting beyond borders. So let us reflect for a moment on what we would do if we faced the same circumstances. The man in the ski mask has just invited us to ask him about himself. How should we respond to his invitation? How can we deal with his anger and suspicion? How do we deal with our *own* fear and confusion? If our lives and the lives of others depended on the words we chose, how exactly would we respond?

Instinctively, Picco searched for common ground.

'Do you have children?' he asked.

'Yes,' the man replied.

'So do I,' Picco replied. 'And are you doing this because you want to give your children a better world?'

'Of course.'

'Well, I am too. So it turns out that we are both fathers who want to give our children a better world.'

The man in the ski mask quietly shifted. He leaned toward Picco, peering directly into his face.

'Where the hell do you come from?' he asked with intense curiosity.

Reflecting on this life-and-death conversation years later, Picco told me that this initial conversation 'blew the man in the ski mask out of his chair'. Picco had chosen the right language, at the right time, to bring his adversary into a relationship. They had, in a word, connected.

With consummate skill, Picco began to create a shared context with his captor. Beyond all their deep differences and the conflicting political views, Picco and his captor had discovered at least one common identity: they were devoted fathers. Even though it would have been easier for both the 'terrorist' and the 'diplomat' to remain walled off from each other inside those one-dimensional identities, they both stepped out of those narrow, separate cells and found common ground. Instead of reacting out of fear, they connected out of curiosity. Their conversation, which eventually led to the release of the hostages, required courage from both men.

'Why did you begin the conversation this way?' I asked Picco during our interview.

'Each of us has multiple identities,' he explained. 'Each of us is more than one thing. I knew that was true for me, and also that it must be true for the man in the ski mask. I knew that finding an identity that we had in common would build a bridge.'

'Please say more about bridging,' I probed. 'What exactly is involved?'

'It was clear when I was brought into their hideout that they thought I was from a different planet. My first challenge was to overcome that notion; otherwise I would get nowhere. Discovering that we were both fathers who cared about our children was the first step. It changed the dynamic between us. I believe that these first few exchanges are what opened the door to a successful negotiation.'

Ever since that fateful night, Picco has been an ardent student of how to connect across borders.

'Our global awareness is rooted in a recognition of multiple identities,' he explained. 'Nation states project the illusion of single identities. But it is not the truth. To be "French" or "South African" is not a monolithic, uniform identity. I believe that this illusion of single identity is at the core of conflict. We must break out of this box. And I am alive today because I did so.'

'So you do not like being called "Italian"?' I ask him.

'I won't even tolerate a *series* of adjectives,' he replies. 'We're so complex that one word is both an inadequate and a pretentious way to describe who we are. The word "Italian" simply doesn't capture who I am. There are fifty million Italians. We're all different from each other.'

'What other adjectives would you use?' I ask him.

'Oh my, oh my,' he says, and falls silent. 'I don't even know where to begin.' Since he cannot find the words to say, he decides instead to tell me a story.

'It was 1975. I was in Cyprus, which was already divided. I was having my first conversation with a Turkish official. He was a stern military man, and I was young and lacked confidence. I was not sure how I would manage to build rapport with him.

' "Where are you from?" the Turkish officer asked me.

' "From Italy," I replied.

' "Ahhhh," he said, breaking into a smile. "We are both *Mediterraneans.*" '

Picco paused for a moment and looked at me. He let the final word hang silently in the air before he put it into words.

'I am actually alive because I have accepted the reality of

multiple identities,' Picco continued, his voice filled with emotion. 'If we live in a xenophobic culture, which demands that we all pretend to be the same, it is very hard to see this reality. To be global citizens, we must break out of the straitjacket of single identity.'

'What happens if we don't free ourselves?' I asked him.

'Then you will always create enemies.'

'*Create* enemies?' I asked to draw him out. 'Aren't the enemies real?'

'That some of the leaders in the West have framed the issue of our relationship with the Middle East in cold-war terms was a huge mistake. The frame is fundamentally incorrect. "The West" and "the Islamic world" is the wrong frame. The frame implies that all Muslims are in one group, and all Westerners are in another. But nothing could be further from the truth. The dividing line is *not* Muslims versus the West. It is extremists versus everybody else. Framing this issue incorrectly has pushed a lot of people into Osama bin Laden's camp who do not want to be there.'

According to opinion polls, this is one of the undesired impacts of the arrogant language and ignorant attitudes that shaped recent American foreign policy and consequently bred such distrust of American motives. The consequence, in Picco's words, is a 'canyon' between America and the Middle East similar to the one that existed during the cold war between East and West.

Not long ago I was at a conference with Satish Kumar, the well-known Indian-born editor of *Resurgence* magazine, when he heard someone refer to 'the border that divides India from Pakistan'.

'Ah, my friend,' he interrupted. 'I do not know that border. I only know the border that *connects* India *to* Pakistan.'

The truth is: any border that *divides* us – geographical, economic, linguistic, religious, cultural, etc. – can also be a border that *connects* us. But first we have to change our point of view.

Fortunately, the Citizen 5.0 within each of us knows instinctively that there are ways to deal with differences. Whether we use this capacity to help our business expand into new markets or to bring a peace to a war-torn country, it is the most precious of all human resources. As global citizens, it is time for us to mine for this resource with the same passion that we dig for gold or oil.

In the following pages, let is look more closely at the different skills that make connecting possible. They include: (1) asking questions that open up new possibilities; (2) witnessing the multiple identities that make ourselves and others fully human; (3) being willing to truly listen to others, even if we do not like what we hear; (4) using communications media to find common ground, not to judge; (5) having the discipline to meet with and listen to our enemies; and (6) responding to injustice by seeking reconciliation rather than revenge. Let us explore each of these dimensions of connecting more closely.

● ● ● ● ● ● ● ● ● ● ● ● ● ●

🌐 Hebrew University and Palestinian Refugee Camp, Jerusalem. 2002.

Nadera is a rarity: a Palestinian woman who is a full professor at an Israeli university. As we speak in the faculty club at one of Israel's most prestigious universities, she offers to take me on a research trip to a Palestinian refugee camp. Over the years she has had to learn to move between the poor, disenfranchised, less educated, and often angry communities of the Palestinian minority and the wealthy, powerful, highly educated communities of Israeli Jews.

In less than ten minutes, we arrive in a refugee camp where Nadera begins interviewing mothers whose children have been incarcerated by Israeli police. As we listen to Palestinian mothers whose children have been beaten and tortured by what they view as an occupying army, her face records not only her compassion, but her own deep pain.

Nadera meets these mothers around a table in a day-care centre. When the mothers complain to the soldiers about how they treat their children, the soldiers hide behind the law. Some are decent; others are brutal. 'The brutal ones tell us,' says one mother, 'that the children are not ours. "It is your job to raise them," they say, "and our job to kill them." '

Nadera's compassion is monitored on both sides with suspicion. On the one hand, her Palestinian friends chastise her for being too friendly with the Jews. ('Look where your "cousins" have driven their tanks today!' one of them said to her not long ago, after the Israeli army invaded yet another town in the occupied territories.) On the other hand, some of her Jewish colleagues at the university are alarmed by the 'political' nature of her research and have advised her, usually in a whisper, that publishing it might prevent her from getting tenure.

Nadera refuses to give in to the easy hatred that is present on both sides – refuses to cut her world in half. Instead, even after suffering physical violence and repeated threats, she continues to be true to her vision of an Israel that treats all its citizens equally.

● ● ● ● ● ● ● ● ● ● ● ● ● ● ●

When we fail to connect with our neighbours and instead act on stereotypes, we build walls that do not have to exist. We create a monolithic, uniform 'us' which often gives rise to an equally monolithic, uniform 'them'. Both, in fact, are illusions – and the price we pay for this illusion is often lethally high. We revert to Citizen 1.0–2.0.

While flying across the Atlantic on Air Force One in mid-2008, a reporter asked then President George W. Bush if he regretted any mistakes that he had made regarding his administration's military actions in the Middle East. 'I think that in retrospect I could have used a different tone, a different rhetoric,' he replied.

He was referring to his macho-sounding challenge to al-Qa'eda to 'bring 'em on' and his Wild West pledge that he would get Osama bin Laden 'dead or alive'. He regretted those phrases, he said, because they 'indicated to people that I was, you know, not a man of peace.'[1]

It took five years of brutal war in Iraq to enable President Bush to learn that communication without connection does not work. When we fail to recognize the complexity of the Other, then the real Technicolor world becomes a black-and-white, 'you're-with-us-or-against-us' storyboard for a political fantasy.

When Geert Wilders, a Dutch Member of Parliament, decided to produce the video *Fitna*, he claimed his intention was to raise awareness about the challenges posed by an increasing Muslim presence in Europe. When the film generated a wave of fury among the followers of Islam, including death threats, Wilders blamed his audience for misunderstanding his message. But if you watch *Fitna* closely, as millions of people around the world have done, you will see a style of communication that lacks connection. Instead of creating common ground, *Fitna* eliminates it.[2]

In his well-produced, incendiary documentary, Wilders takes a series of warlike passages from the Koran and juxtaposes them with video clips showing the most paranoid, vicious, and often anti-Semitic statements from a variety of adult Arabic-looking speakers. (The only exception is one scene in which a young Arabic child is being taught that, according to the Koran, all Jews are 'apes and pigs'.) The result is a short powerful film that showcases the strand of thinking within the Muslim community that preaches violence against non-Muslims and justifies the most heinous acts by invoking the name of Allah. If you watch it, you will see how effectively it triggers an emotional response. That response is not connection, or love. It is disconnection, or hate.

Devout Muslims were of course shocked and outraged by *Fitna*. The Arab press throughout the world denounced the film. Some Muslim leaders advocated that Wilders be assassinated, as they had with the author Salman Rushdie. Scores of counter-videos emerged on the Web attempting to refute the arguments made in the film.[3]

'I am not saying all Muslims are wrong or are terrorists or criminals,' Wilders explained in one his rare interviews with the press, in an effort to dispel accusations that he is a racist. Pleading innocence, he assured his interviewer that he does not hate all Muslims, but rather simply wanted to point out that Islam is, in his words, 'retarded' and 'dangerous'. The purpose of *Fitna*, he explained, was to warn his fellow Dutch citizens that 'Islam and the Koran are dangers to the preservation of freedom in the Netherlands.'

What makes Wilders' way of communicating so destructive is that its purpose is not to connect, but to judge. By sharing a small, twisted, and highly toxic 'part' of the Koran, combined with excerpts of speeches from the most virulent and hate-filled

Muslim speakers, he feeds the viewer's prejudice against Islam. By harnessing the Citizen 2.0 mentality in each of us, he inspires us to regress into our narrowest and most hateful identity.

When Wilders was invited by the United Kingdom Independence Party to screen his film in London, the British government detained him at Heathrow airport, informed him that he posed a threat to public safety, and forced him to take the next flight back to the Netherlands. Wilders responded by calling Prime Minister Gordon Brown 'the biggest coward in Europe', providing further evidence that he responds to conflict by resorting to insults. Instead of making him a 'free speech martyr' by banning him from entering their country, the British government might have been wiser to protect his civic right to make a fool of himself.[4]

As any thoughtful student of the Abrahamic faiths knows, one can find violent, racist passages in the Bible and Talmud as well as the Koran. A documentary filmmaker would have no trouble stringing together random ravings from Jewish and Christian extremists who spew fear and hatred against Muslims. Indeed, such ideological trash-talk from virtually every faith tradition can be found on the Web with frightening ease.

Instead of making a boundary-crossing film about religious fanaticism, Wilders made a product that implies that only Islam suffers from this illness. By portraying the almost universal human tendency to hate the Other as a problem solely of Islam, he fed the myth that only violent, extremist Islam threatens civilization. In fact, violent pseudo-religious extremism in *any* faith poses such a threat.

To put it starkly, *Wilders used words and images to build a wall; global citizens use them to build a bridge.* That we human beings know how to communicate for peace and understanding is clear.

We have the skills. The question is: why don't we use them more often – and more skilfully?

To his lasting credit, President Barack Obama tried to build a bridge between the Muslim world and the US in his historic speech in Cairo on 4 June 2009. Instead of showcasing the worst of Islam as evil and implying that Jews and Christians were innocent, he called on people of all the Abrahamic faiths to draw on the best of their unique heritages. 'We have the power to make the world we seek,' he said to an audience that included millions throughout the world, 'but only if we have the courage to make a new beginning . . . ' And then, in an unprecedented step for a US leader, he quoted respectfully from the holy books of the three great Western religions:

> The Holy Koran tells us: 'O mankind! We have created
>   you male and female; and we have made you into
>   nations and tribes so that you may know one another.'
> The Talmud tells us: 'The whole of the Torah is for the
>   purpose of promoting peace.'
> The Holy Bible tells us: 'Blessed are the peacemakers, for
>   they shall be called sons of God.'

After waiting for his applauding Egyptian audience to quiet, he concluded: 'The people of the world can live together in peace. We know that is God's vision. Now that must be our work here on Earth.'

By challenging Jews to empathize with Palestinians, and Muslims to empathize with Israelis, Obama demonstrated his care for *both* sides – and invited them to co-create a 'new beginning'. To the best of his ability, he used language to connect.[5]

● ● ● ● ● ● ● ● ● ● ● ● ●

🌐 New Delhi, India. December 1969.

Because the blow to my head from the accident left me suffering from amnesia, my first memory was of lying on a table, looking up at a man with a greying beard and a white turban. He was pointing a small sharp knife straight at my head.

Shocked, I grabbed the turbaned man's arm and asked him to identify himself. Although he replied that he was a surgeon, I was suspicious. The surroundings in the room did not resemble a hospital. The so-called 'doctor' was not dressed in a surgical gown. The floor was dirty. Virtually no medical equipment was on hand. Most disturbing of all, the man standing by the door wearing a long muddy overcoat and carrying a long rifle was dressed more like a mountain bandit than a security guard.

'You must let me operate – and quickly,' said the man with the knife. 'You must let me release the pressure of blood under your skin, or your brain might haemorrhage. I need to do this right now – or you might die.'

At precisely the time when I needed to be fully aware, I was in shock. Just when I needed to think clearly, my brain was deranged. At the very moment when I faced a life-and-death decision, I was paranoid.

Triggered by the trauma of the head wound, my mind began spinning out a paranoid tale: I had been brought to this building by the driver who had hit our car, who was at fault, and who had asked these people to assassinate me so that I could not press charges or testify against him.

Fortunately, after some further conversation and staring deeply into the surgeon's kind eyes, I agreed to let him operate. If I had given into my paranoia, I would not be alive today.

● ● ● ● ● ● ● ● ● ● ● ● ● ● ●

To feel fear is human. Fear is an emotion that protects us from danger. But paranoia is different. It does not protect us but rather isolates and, ultimately, endangers us. Global citizens must be vigilant about the paranoid purveyors of hate and paranoia that fill the airwaves and Websites. The examples used here are about videos circulating in Europe and the USA; but virtually every culture in the world is experiencing a similar struggle. In this globalizing world, each of us must choose to open or close our hearts.

In the midst of the 2008 US presidential election, I found in my mailbox a small package. On it, in large black letters, was the word 'OBSESSION', but instead of the letter 'O' there was the crescent moon and star that symbolizes Islam, and part of the final 'N' was an assault rifle. Inside the package was a DVD showing a man in an Arab headdress, followed by other men carrying weapons – a 'gift' sent by the Clarion Fund, an under-the-radar organization that has carefully camouflaged its leaders and funders. Its tagline, however, made clear its intentions: 'national security through education.'[6]

When I put the DVD in my computer and pushed play, the full title appeared on the screen: Obsession: Radical Islam's War against the West. The first words that scrolled across the screen explained that this is a film about 'radical Islamic terror'. The video, which according to its publicity was sent to twenty-eight million American homes, was filled with words and images designed to convey one message: Islam equals terrorism.[7]

I share information about this film and its website because

global citizens need to be aware of these insidious communication strategies and learn how to counteract them. It is not enough for high-minded global citizens to preach love; we must also study hate. We must face this human emotion squarely, both in others and in ourselves. If we are to truly celebrate the light of the world, we must also face its darkness.

The global media landscape is filled with communication that distorts rather than educates, that disconnects rather than connects, that closes rather than opens our hearts. We can fill our minds with products like *Fitna* and *Obsession*, and other films that dehumanize other human beings. Or we can listen to those who teach us, by word and by example, that 'us' and 'them' are part of a single, if often fragmented, family.

● ● ● ● ● ● ● ● ● ● ● ● ● ● ●

◉ Constitution Center. Philadelphia, Pennsylvania. 18 March 2008.

'We the people of the United States, in order to form a perfect union . . . ' Senator Barack Obama said from behind the podium. He had chosen this site, where the Founding Fathers had declared the birth of a nation, to give a speech addressing the highly charged subject of race relations in America. He had chosen this moment to address the issue that was threatening to derail his campaign to become the first African-American President of the United States of America.

His staff was divided about whether he should make this televised address. Some felt it was drawing too much attention to the issue of race. Others felt that it risked losing more votes than it would gain. But his key advisers agreed with the senator that the time had come to speak his mind.

Linguists and political scientists soon began analysing the speech to understand its power. From the opening words of the US constitution to the closing story about an old black man inspired by a young white woman, Obama's speech evoked the connections that keep Americans united. 'I have brothers, sisters, nieces, nephews, uncles, and cousins of every race and every hue, scattered across three continents,' he said. His pride in his diverse heritage shone through his face, and invited his listeners to reflect on their own complex ancestry.

Obama explained the legitimate reasons why some older black Americans like him were often bitter and resentful towards whites. But with equal compassion, he also explained why some white Americans were bitter and resentful toward racial minorities.

In the days following the speech, a miracle – fleeting but real – happened in America. Even in the intensely partisan atmosphere of the election season, Senator Obama had connected with the American people on a subject that has haunted the country since the Civil War. From right-wing TV commentators to left-wing activists, citizens of all political persuasions and all races heralded the speech as a turning point in the election.[8]

● ● ● ● ● ● ● ● ● ● ● ● ● ● ●

When we, as global citizens, listen to candidates who seek to persuade us to support them, we must learn to listen between the lines. When a speech is heralded as 'great' or 'historic' by people throughout a nation and the world, it is worth reflecting on why. What is it about that leader's way of speaking that cuts through the divisive, polarized atmosphere of modern elections and reaches across the political spectrum to touch so many diverse constituencies? What enables it to connect?

In my view, the common denominator is that the speakers have reached deep enough into themselves to touch some aspect of the universal root of human experience. They appeal to what unites us, not what divides us. They evoke the deeper sense of connection that is beneath all the surface feelings of separation. They dig deeply to the root and avoid the divisive, 'partisan' surface.

Just as Mahatma Gandhi appealed to Britons' sense of justice, and Nelson Mandela appealed to white South Africans' sense of fairness, so did Obama appeal to Americans' sense of equality. Like other great bridge-builders before him, Obama began with the core universal values that all Americans profess to share. He called his speech 'A More Perfect Union', and appealed to his listeners to create it with him.

In his way of speaking, Obama embodied an open heart. Regarding angry black Americans who had suffered under racial segregation, police brutality, lynchings, and denial of human rights, Obama said: 'That anger is not always productive . . . But the anger is real; it is powerful; and to simply wish it away, to condemn it without understanding its roots, only serves to widen the chasm of misunderstanding that exists between the races.' Regarding resentful white Americans who feel left behind by change, anxious about their future, and suspicious about special treatment of minorities, Obama said with equal compassion: 'Their experience is the immigrant experience – as far as they're concerned, no one's handed them anything . . . So when they are told to bus their children to a school across town; when they hear that an African-American is getting an advantage in landing a good job or a spot in a good college . . . when they're told that their fears about crime in urban neighbourhoods are somehow prejudiced, resentment builds over time.'

But after empathizing with both races, he challenged both black and white (and Latina and Asian) to transcend the past and build on 'the true genius of this nation'. When he was asked the following day by a reporter what he meant by 'patriotism', he did not speak about the flag, or fighting enemies, or being progressive rather than conservative. He began his definition with 'caring about one another'. And by the way he expressed that caring, Obama connected to both blacks *and* whites, right and left, old and young.

● ● ● ● ● ● ● ● ● ● ● ● ● ●

🌐 Chicago Restaurant. Late September 2001.

'You realize, don't you, that the political dynamics have changed,' said the veteran media consultant to the young politician, whose once promising career was now in trouble.

'What do you mean?' asked the politician, even though he already knew the answer. There on the front of the page of the *Chicago Tribune*, filled with post 9-11 stories, was the latest picture of Osama bin Laden.

'Really bad luck,' said the media consultant. 'You can't change your name . . . Maybe if you were at the start of your career, you know, you could use a nickname or something. But now . . . '

It was a depressing end to a lunch. The media consultant clearly believed that with the middle name 'Hussein', Barack Obama's career was over.[9]

● ● ● ● ● ● ● ● ● ● ● ● ● ●

All our identities cross borders. Each of us is many parts woven together. Are we not all mixtures of complex lineages – with many identities, allegiances, and selves? Are we not all somehow patched together? No matter what external borders we may choose to cross, we all must learn to cross these internal borders. We can connect with others only to the degree that we can connect to our multiple selves.

Instead of thinking in tired, worn-out terms that lump millions, sometimes hundreds of millions, of people into simplistic categories, global citizens can acknowledge our own and others' complexity. This shift from abstraction to humanness is a key to connecting – and to global citizenship itself.

Notice, for example, what image comes to your mind when you read the words 'Arab man'. Unless you are from an Arab country, or have many male Arab friends, the image is an abstraction, or at best a composite. You have only imagined a category, not a person. You still do not know who he is. To know him, you must go beyond this stereotype and enter the three-dimensional, flesh-and-blood world.

To bring this point alive, let me introduce you to a specific 'Arab man'. His name is Amin Maalouf. Within moments of meeting him, you will require your first of many hyphens. Maalouf is a *Lebanese*-Arab. He comes from a country that has been a crossroads in the Middle East, a country with a proud but troubled past.

As you get to know him, you will find that he is a *Christian*-Lebanese-Arab. His family is from the mountainous region of southern Lebanon, which has been Christian and Arab since the second or third century. So if your stereotype of 'Arab man' assumed that he was a Muslim as well, think again: there are tens of millions of Christian Arabs scattered around the world.

A Lebanese Catholic educated in a French school by Jesuit fathers, Maalouf has for many years been a resident and citizen of France. So he is *French*-Christian-Lebanese-Arab. He is part of the Lebanese diaspora, one of scores of seismic shifts in human population that have intermixed humanity.[10]

And if this series of adjectives is not enough to begin stretching our minds, Maalouf reminds us that he had family members who were Protestant, a Turkish grandmother, and a grandfather who was a poet and who wanted nothing to do with any religion. So behind the stereotype 'Arab man', we discover a multifaceted human being, just as complex and real as we are.

'How many of my fellow men share with me all the different elements that have shaped my identity and determined the main outlines of my life?' Maalouf pointedly asks in his brilliant essay *Les Identités meurtrières* (translated into English and published as *In The Name of Identity: Violence and the Need to Belong*). 'There's no need to go on. I'll merely say: very few. Perhaps none at all. And that is what I want to emphasize: through each one of my affiliations, taken *separately*, I possess a certain kinship with a large number of my fellow human beings; but because of all these allegiances, taken *together*, I possess my own identity, completely different from any other.'[11]

Put simply, Amin Maalouf is one of a kind – and so are you and I. Therefore, every time we lump people together in huge categories like 'Western Christians' or 'Arab Muslims' we are using language in a way that stereotypes. For global citizens, such stereotypes are a dead end. They prevent witnessing, undermine learning, and make connecting impossible. At the very worst, they help pave the way to war and genocide.[12]

The tendency to turn our enemies into less-than-human stereotypes has scarred recent history. You can recognize this kind of leadership by analysing the strategies of the most infamous dictators and tyrants, who have always dehumanized the Other. Hitler's right-hand man, Hermann Goering, admitted this at the Nuremberg trials. For leaders, Goering said, 'it is always a simple matter to drag the people along'. Regardless of the type of political system, he believed that 'the people can always be brought to the bidding of the leaders'. His strategy was simple: 'All you have to do is tell them they are being attacked, and denounce the peacemakers for lack of patriotism and exposing the country to danger. *It works the same in any country.*'

'I *believed* the propaganda that all Jews were criminals and subhumans and that they were the cause of Germany's decline after the First World War,' admitted Kurt Mobius, an officer at the Chelmo concentration camp, one of the more candid Nazi defendants at Nuremberg. 'The thought that one should disobey or evade the order to participate in the extermination of the Jews did not therefore enter my mind at all.' [13]

The dehumanization, paranoia, and cruelty that are the three pillars of genocide only further underscore the power of connecting. As long as we maintain some positive human ties between 'us' and 'them', as long as we say 'no' to the black-and-white simplifiers who turn 'our side' into angels and 'their side' into demons, such insanity is impossible.

This is not only good diplomacy; it is good business. In a competitive marketplace, who is more likely to win a client – the narrow-minded, culture-bound Citizen 3.0 or the more creative, connective Citizen 4.0–5.0?

When I first met engineer Chris van Note, I was impressed by the vast geographic range of his work. He has created major international projects such as airports in a wide range of cultures from East and West Africa, Turkey, Taiwan, Venezuela, Serbia,

Mexico, the Dominican Republic, and Spain. So I was naturally curious about what he had learned that engineers working within a single culture might not have.

'In your field,' I asked him, 'what makes someone successful internationally? Why did you get these jobs, not your competitors?'

'In my opinion,' Chris replied, 'the single most important attribute that can help lead to success on international projects is a person's ability to connect to others from different cultures. This, of course, depends on one's *desire* to connect. If there is no desire to connect to people who may be very different than you are, then there will not likely be a true connection.'

'But why do some people in your profession have the *desire* to connect while others don't?'

'Curiosity has something to do with it,' Chris said, after a moment's pause. 'Picture two engineers from the American Midwest who have never been abroad or never conducted any international business dealings. They are both trying to develop their competing businesses in Turkey.

'One engineer reads several books on Turkey, studies the local news to understand what is going on in the country, learns to speak some words and phrases in the local languages, obtains Department of State information on the country, sets up a meeting in advance with the local commercial attaché in Istanbul to learn what he can prior to his business meetings, and becomes aware of the current political tensions within the country.

'The other engineer does nothing to prepare. He gets on the plane not having pre-learned anything about Turkey.

'Which of these two engineers do you think has a better chance of success? Who will make a better first impression? Who will have the competitive edge?'

Clearly, connecting involves respect. Effective diplomats or executives who work all over the world have learned to respect people despite their cultural differences. Although demagogic politicians can succeed by fanning the flames of fear and hatred, successful business people cannot. They *must* connect.

In the private sector, CEOs succeed by turning people who are different from themselves into *customers*, not *enemies*. So it is not surprising that the world's leading companies have found ways of connecting across borders that have far outpaced their counterparts in government. Corporate leaders use the motivation of profit, not just principle, to solve the riddle of human connection. Exploring how they connect to their global customers provides us a compelling case study of how to connect across borders.

To achieve global sales, global companies often engage in a process called 'localization'. Now almost everyone has heard the word 'globalization', but for some reason few of us are as familiar with 'localization'. The two terms, in fact, go together hand-in-glove. In specific businesses, such as software, the contemporary meaning of localization is very specific. It refers to the process of adapting programs to linguistic and regional differences. It is a common mistake to think that software – for example, Microsoft Windows – can be used throughout the world without major modifications other than translation. In fact, Bill Gates himself made this mistake.

When Microsoft began selling globally to non-English-speaking markets, the company was faced with runaway cost increases. It found itself faced with more than a thousand 'localization projects' annually. At first, Gates could not understand why localization was so complex, and so expensive. He thought adapting his company's products to different cultures – in other words, localization – should be straight-forward. It's 'just a linguistic process', he told his global marketing team impatiently.

Well, Gates was wrong. Selling Microsoft products globally was far, far more than just a linguistic challenge. He finally realized how wrong he was when he saw the budget for product localization. Fully two-thirds of the localization costs did not involve translation at all, but re-engineering, testing, and project management.

The executive who helped Gates understand the problem, and fix it, was David Brooks, Microsoft's senior director of international product strategy. The challenge Brooks faced was what he calls the 'US-centric mentality of the [software] development community', including his famous boss.

Now someone calling the American Department of Defense or the White House 'US-centric' is not surprising. But what does it mean when a top Microsoft executive applies that term to software engineers?

According to Brooks, core software-development teams comprised mostly of Americans 'paid little attention to international issues'. They held a naive, culturally limited view that 'localization equals translation' and were 'unaware of the biases and engineering limitations inherent in the US product they were building.'

The example Brooks cites is the codepage. In English, the number of characters and other symbols totalled 256. Each item requires one byte. By contrast, in Japanese there are thousands of symbols, and each requires two bytes. If a Microsoft product were to use single-byte encoding (as did the original American versions), the Japanese version would have to be rebuilt from scratch.

The solution, as Microsoft and other companies that decided

to 'go global' learned, was to eliminate these problems at the source – that is, in the core code itself. So, in the example cited above, Microsoft opted for a double-byte codepage so that the software could accommodate all languages.[14]

If you look beneath the surface details of this rather technical case study from the computer software industry, you will find embedded within it a fable worthy of Aesop. The moral of the tale is that it is better to understand the full scope and significance of global differences early rather than late. Understood late, leaders find themselves playing a costly game of infinite modifications and mistakes; understood early, leaders can create a strategy that incorporates and transcends differences and spread their message far and wide.

In other words, connecting is not only good foreign policy. It is good business. Learning to connect can clinch a business deal, increase global sales – and sometimes even save a life.

* * * * * * * * * * * * * *

🌐 Seeds of Peace Camp. Otisfield, Maine. August 2002.

'Why did you attend the Seeds of Peace Camp?' I asked Ariel, a slender, light-skinned Jew who lives in a small settlement at the edge of Jerusalem.

'I came to win arguments,' he remembers. 'Like most first-year campers, I could not accept the other side. I wanted to win.'

'And why did you come back the second year?'

'Like many others, I came back to listen. I realized that winning arguments accomplishes nothing.'

* * * * * * * * * * * * * *

Listening (sometimes called 'deep listening') is a vital survival skill, the first and most practical line of self-defence in a dangerous world. Yet many conventional leaders don't use it. Particularly in times of crisis, they just speak louder and broadcast farther. If our home country is powerful and prominent on the world stage, we will hear criticism. Do we have the courage to listen – or do we simply 'tune out?'

Truly listening to criticism of one's culture or one's country is an essential part of creating relationships. Connecting depends not only on knowing how to talk across borders. It also means knowing how to listen across borders. The other core skills – reading, writing, and speaking – are all taught in schools. But listening is rarely taught or studied because it is so profoundly undervalued.

To be a global citizen requires respecting people different from ourselves, and who know what we don't. Only by connecting with others who hold divergent views, and truly listening to what they have to say, can we evolve into global citizens.

Even though business texts on sales, on management, and on negotiation cite 'learning to listen' as a basic ingredient of success,[15] listening is often considered to be as simple as having ears. In fact, listening is harder than talking. Unlike ordinary speech, which is little more than an expression of one's own point of view, true listening involves empathy: entering into the perspective of another human being. While this may be taught in school-based education, a framed diploma hanging on one's wall does not mean one knows how to listen. On the contrary, it is usually learned through being humbled by experience.

Since we live in a world where technology allows words and images to reach people on the other side of the world, we might as well develop the communication 'software' that will put the hardware to good use. Otherwise, we will, to paraphrase Thomas Friedman, use all the tools for broadcasting words but none of the tools for understanding. Nothing builds understanding and trust more reliably than listening. Nothing depletes trust more than failing to do so.

How strange it is, then, that we think of 'leadership' more in terms of speaking brilliantly, not listening deeply. This is in part because we become aware of leaders only when they have emerged on the world stage and are asked to give speeches in front of large crowds. Particularly because of the media, we never get to know the 'listener' inside the 'speaker'. When leaders such as Nelson Mandela or Barack Obama become renowned, television portrays them delivering lectures at prestigious forums or speaking charismatically in front of huge rallies. But they did not become leaders solely through brilliant oratory. For example, Mandela's 'long walk to freedom' was based on listening. 'As a leader,' Mandela wrote, 'I have always endeavoured to listen to what each and every person in a discussion had to say before venturing my own opinion. Oftentimes, my own opinion will simply represent a consensus of what I have heard in the discussion.'[16] The same applies to Obama: as those close to him will attest, he listens even better than he speaks.

Obama's and Mandela's rise to power underscores the profound power of listening. It meets the universal need to be understood and recognized. It creates a safe, welcoming environment in which real issues can be addressed. And it increases the chances that the full resources of everyone will emerge. At its best, deep and heartful listening is a 'moral beacon', one that empowers as well as illumines. It is the material from which bridges of connection are built.[17]

●●●●●●●●●●●●●●●

🌐 Robben Island. Off the coast of Cape Town, South Africa. April 2002.

'Where are you from?' asks the tour guide, a middle-aged black man named P.T.

'Uganda,' answers one man in a business suit.

'Sweden,' answer two young women.

'Johannesburg,' says a father with two young children.

'Spain,' replies a young couple, who look like they are on their honeymoon.

'We're from England,' says the apparent leader of a small group of men, all members of a travelling soccer team.

'New Zealand,' says a mother with her family.

'The whole world is here in this prison today,' observes P.T. 'Thank you all for coming. I learned a lot here, and I am sure you will too.'

As people nod their heads, P.T. explains that he himself had been a prisoner. His identification number was 38/54. For the crime of being a student leader in the struggle against apartheid, he was brought to Robben Island to serve a fifteen-year sentence. Thanks to the abolition of apartheid, P.T. served less than half his sentence before being set free.

After walking through the maze of the prison, I am disoriented. I cannot remember where the exit is located. It is then that I am struck by the fact that a former prisoner is my guide. He is telling us about a group of men who turned Section C into a think-tank that designed the future of a country. The prison was their university, and now it is ours. We have come to a prison to learn about freedom.

●●●●●●●●●●●●●●●

Nowhere has the challenge of connecting played a more vital role than in South Africa. When apartheid ended, the challenge of responding to its injustices was put to the test in a way that it had never been tested before. Instead of adopting the Nuremberg model, where those accused of war crimes were tried and (if found guilty) punished, the Truth and Reconciliation Commission, under the leadership of Archbishop Desmond Tutu, decided that its first priority was not punishment but truth. The Commission did not want the guilty to be convicted; they wanted the guilty to take responsibility for their actions and to be witnessed.

According to Tutu, there were two major reasons why the Commission sought reconciliation not retribution. The first was that South Africa was trying to avoid a war, not to convict criminals from a war that had already happened. Even though many observers were convinced that apartheid would never end in South Africa without a blood bath, they were fortunately wrong. Because war was avoided, there was no 'victor' who could impose justice on the 'vanquished'. According to Archbishop Tutu: 'In South Africa, where we had a military stalemate, that was clearly an impossible option. Neither side in the struggle (the state nor the liberation movement) had defeated the other and hence nobody was in a position to enforce a so-called victor's justice.' For a country still on the brink of civil war to undertake a criminal process of punishing its own 'war criminals' would be fratricidal, and potentially catastrophic.

But the second reason was even more important. The Commission believed that, in the circumstances facing their country, 'the criminal justice system is not the best way to determine the truth. There is no incentive for perpetrators to tell the truth and often the court must decide between the word of one victim against the evidence of many perpetrators.' Because the Commission believed that only the truth would truly set the nation free, they were willing to sacrifice the desire to punish on behalf of their deeper desire to witness the sometimes terrible yet liberating, story of their own past.[18]

Again and again, when President Nelson Mandela challenged his fellow citizens to 'Build a better South Africa for All!' he would evoke this tradition of *ubuntu* – of recognizing the common humanity that transcends all differences. Perhaps that is the single word that most eloquently captures the essence of connecting, for it embraces more than just what *I* am. It celebrates what *we* are.

● ● ● ● ● ● ● ● ● ● ● ● ● ● ●

◉ Gorkarna Forest Resort. Kathmandu, Nepal. September 2009.

'The water wars have already begun,' says my Nepali colleague, a high-level official in the Ministry of Irrigation. 'Unless we find a new way of dealing with this conflict, it will be a crisis beyond our imagining.'

A major conference is underway here about the impact of climate change on the Himalayan watershed, which – according to a growing scientific consensus – is experiencing a radical and rapid decrease in glacial ice. This means that the more than two *billion* people who depend on this watershed for their fresh water supplies will find themselves in an intensifying struggle for this dwindling resource.

'What do you think we can do to deal with this crisis?' I ask my colleague.

'I don't know,' he admits frankly. 'But I *do* know that we can't solve the problem in the old ways. We have to come together – all the thirteen nations that rely on this water supply – and recognize that we are in the same boat. Nepal can lead the way – but not if we are trapped in a civil war!'

• • • • • • • • • • • • • •

In April 2008, former President Carter was in Nepal to monitor its historic elections, which included the former Maoists who had ignited a civil war. Many of the objectives of the revolutionaries had been achieved: the monarchy had been abolished; discrimination against untouchables had been outlawed; a democratic republic with free elections had been established. In only two years, the 'rebels' had become successful politicians, and, after their victory in the election, had become full partners in drafting a new constitution.

Carter was en route to the Middle East for a controversial meeting with the 'extremist Muslim' group Hamas. It was controversial because the Bush administration had criticized Carter for talking to all sides. In addition to meeting with the Palestinian 'terrorist' organization Hamas, Carter told the press: 'We'll be meeting with the Israelis. We'll be meeting with Fatah [another Palestinian political party]. We'll be meeting with the Syrians, the Egyptians, the Jordanians, the Saudi Arabians, and with the whole gamut of people who might have to play a crucial role in any future peace agreement that involves the Middle East.'[19]

Unlike the Bush administration, Carter believed that connecting is essential to communication, and that meeting outlaw groups like Hamas can eventually lead to their participation in the democratic process. 'In the Middle East, as in Nepal,' Carter wrote after returning home to Georgia, 'the path to peace lies in negotiation, not in isolation.'[20]

It is not always the right decision to talk with one's enemy. But it is definitely not a 'global citizen's' strategy to refuse to talk with them under any circumstances. Since almost two out of three Israelis favour direct negotiations with Hamas, it seems strange that most US politicians – securely located across an ocean from the turmoil in the Middle East – are against conducting talks.[24] Perhaps being 'tough' is a luxury that those inside the Washington beltway can afford, but that those who are actually face-to-face with danger cannot.

What is missing in the so-called 'tough on terror' approach, paradoxically, is the courage to sit down and connect with people with whom one disagrees. Instead, the 'tough guys' prefer to sit half a world away in comfortable meeting rooms with people who think like them and then craft diplomatic positions and media messages that, they believe, will advance their country's interests around the world. But these public relationship campaigns have a fundamental problem: *they do not connect*. As Ambassador Henry Crumpton, former CIA operative and State Department counter-terrorism expert, puts it: 'You cannot package a message here [in Washington] and have that resonate' in Afghanistan and Iraq. American politicians, he observes, are 'too Washington D.C.-centric.' This tendency to be 'us-centric' is of course only human. To paraphrase the old saying: what we see depends on where we sit. When Ambassador Crumpton criticizes US policies in the Middle East as too 'Washington-centric', or when Microsoft's David Brooks laments the software development community's 'US-centric mentality', they are describing Citizen 1.0–3.0. At these levels of civic awareness, we are able to see the world only from the perspective of our own self, our group, or our nation. But as we human beings develop our capacity to witness, learn, and connect, our horizons expand. We become able to form genuine problem-solving partnerships with people no matter how different they may be from us, or how far away they may live.

Chapter 4

Geo-Partnering: Working Together

There are no 'Britain-only' or 'Europe-only' or 'American-only' solutions to the global threats and challenges we face . . . global problems require global solutions.

— Prime Minister Gordon Brown

We must find a way to live together as one human family.

— US President Barack Obama

In the summer of 2008, my colleagues and I convened a group of the leading global policy think-tanks from around the world at Oxford University. Our goal was to inspire everyone to begin thinking about 'global policy' less parochially, and more globally.

By the second day, the think-tank chiefs from the more conflicted regions of the world found themselves intrigued by one of their colleagues from a region that was actually experiencing relative peace and prosperity. Dr Stephen Leong, our Malaysian colleague from the Institute of Strategic and International Studies in Kuala Lumpur, responded to their questions by explaining the reasons behind the harmony and prosperity among the ASEAN nations – ten south-east Asian countries with a combined population of more than half a billion people.

'Compared to other regions of the world where neighbouring nations are in constant conflict with each other,' Stephen says proudly, 'I think we are learning to work together quite well – despite our profound differences.'

'What's your secret?' asks an African colleague. 'And have you patented it?'

Stephen laughs. 'Well, I don't know if we have a secret – but a story comes to mind.'

He tells us about the ambitious president of a water desalination company. This businessman goes to Singapore (an island nation with virtually no domestic fresh water supplies) and tells the minister in charge of water that, if Singapore buys twenty of his desalinization plants, it will not longer need to import water from Malaysia. Instead, Singapore can become 'independent'.

'No, thank you,' said the minister. 'In that case, we definitely do not want to purchase any.'

'Why not?' asked the President, puzzled.

'Because we *want* to be dependent on Malaysia – and we *want* them to be dependent on us.'

'But what for?' asked the CEO.

'Because interdependence will make us both stronger – and will help us keep the peace.'

Our group of think-tank leaders from around the world were moved by our Malaysian colleague's story. But then a Russian colleague interjected sceptically: 'I believe that your principle of interdependent partnership may work between *friendly* neighbours, but does it apply to *hostile* neighbours?'

In a word, the answer is yes.

Decade after decade, while the Cuban and American governments continued their cold war, the hurricane experts worked closely to present the loss of property and loss of life. Even while the cold-war politicians continue their war of words, the scientists are geo-partnering across borders. 'For any storm that goes over Cuba, we need their [the Cubans'] observations,' says Max Mayfield, the former head of the National Hurricane Center in Miami. 'And they [the Cuban government] need our data from the aircraft.'[1]

These two stories are both teaching us the same lesson: *we need each other*. Hurricanes, cyclones, earthquakes know no borders. Poverty and affluence live next door to each other: one family has more than enough; their neighbours have too little. Drought and flood occur in the same country. Communities with unemployed youth and communities needing workers exist beside the same border. The only way humanity can forge a sustainable future is for human beings to partner together in new ways across the borders that divide us: in other words, to *geo-partner*.

According to current estimates, if the poorest four-fifths of humanity were to live with the lifestyles of the richest fifth, it would require *four* Earths to sustain all of us. As humanity faces what may prove to be the ultimate survival test in the coming decades, we will need an alchemical power bordering on magic to resolve the riddle of environmental sustainability and economic development.

The fact is: we do not have four Earths. We have only one. And we will need nothing less than collaborative global leadership – or geo-partnering – to make our planet work for all of us and our children.

For millennia human beings have partnered with each other to survive. 'In the long history of humankind,' said Charles Darwin, 'those who learned to collaborate and improvise most effectively have prevailed.'[2] But for most of human history that collaboration has been between 'us' – not with 'them'. We have cooperated closely within tribes and clans, and sometimes within cultures and nations. Today humanity faces challenges that require partnerships across the boundaries that divide human beings from each other.

Geo-partnering is *cross*-boundary collaboration between individuals or groups that are different from each other, who often have a history of mutual mistrust or conflict. It is based on a foundation of precious human qualities such as reciprocity, collaboration, synergy, and bridge-building. Geo-partnering is vitally necessary today because no single nation, no single culture, no single profession, and no single hero on a white horse, can meet the challenges we face. It involves two or more parties, bridging a divide; implies horizontal, not vertical; and evokes a field, not a pyramid. It is Citizen 4.0–5.0 *in action*.

As recent natural calamities revealed, geo-partnering is often a matter of life and death. On the day after the devastating earthquake in Sichuan, China, that claimed a hundred thousand lives and left four hundred thousand injured, a senior Chinese diplomat confided to me: 'For the first time in my country, facts are travelling faster than rumours.'

It was true: Chinese leaders were so shocked by the scale of the destruction that they reached out their hands to the world community and asked for help.

When I arrived in China a few days later, I witnessed a nation in mourning. I was moved by the power that a crisis has to unite a people. Humbly determined to save lives, Chinese authorities eagerly accept the world's assistance. Within days, rescue groups from South Korea, Japan, Singapore, Russia, and even Taiwan arrived to join the rescue effort. Meanwhile, the United States dispatched two US Air Force C-17s filled with supplies, including urgently needed tents and generators.

Only ten days earlier in Burma (Myanmar), the military dictatorship reacted very differently when Cyclone Nargis wreaked havoc on the capital city and the Irrawaddy river delta, killing an estimated hundred thousand people and leaving millions homeless or at risk of starvation and disease. Instead of the grieving process leading to unity and hope, it brought despair and anger. The failure of the government to respond, and their unwillingness to let 'foreigners' help, embittered the Burmese people and appalled the rest of the world.

These divergent responses to these two natural calamities illustrate the power of geo-partnership. No matter how hard we human beings try, we cannot prevent further cyclones or earthquakes – or other mega-crises – from occurring. But the way we respond to these tragedies will make all the difference. If we put up walls, arm ourselves, and blindly try to become 'secure' alone, we will only spread darkness. If we reach out – asking and offering to lend a hand, and finding common security through geo-partnerships – we can spread light.

Geo-partnerships are no longer just the old 'strategic alliances' of the 'major powers'. A handful of old men on either side of the Atlantic can no longer determine the fate of the world. 'If there's just a Roosevelt and Churchill sitting in a room with brandy, that's an easier negotiation,' said President Obama at the G20 conference in London in April 2009. 'But that's not the world we live in . . . Our problems must be dealt with through partnership; our progress must be shared.'[3]

· · · · · · · · · · · · · · ·

🌐 The Carter Center. Atlanta, Georgia. February 2002.

'In Africa, we believe in the principle of reciprocity,' President Joaquim Chissano of Mozambique is saying to the audience overflowing the main conference hall. 'We will do something for you today, and you do something for us tomorrow.'

He spoke of reciprocity as if it were a phenomenon of nature – and human nature – as common and as beautiful as the morning dew. But for many in the audience, the very idea seemed out of place, almost alien.

'But this raises the question,' he continues, 'what do the poor have to give the rich?'

He said the last sentence gently, matter-of-factly, as if it was perfectly ordinary. But the room suddenly became very still. I held my breath, wondering what would happen next, as I turned the question over in my mind.

This distinguished, grey-haired statesman looked out at his audience of more than two hundred influential figures from around the world, all concerned about global poverty, including former President Jimmy Carter and the President of the World Bank, James Wolfensohn. Sensing the discomfort in his audience, Chissano explained: 'In the present world context, where we can no longer isolate the poor, the question is what the poor can offer. If you give the poor nothing, they tend to respond with immigration, instability, and hostility. What is needed is mutual confidence. We in the developing nations have felt a lot of suspicion from the developed nations. We are seeking a new partnership . . . based on a commonality of interests . . . a win–win global economy.'

'What do the poor have to give the rich?' was the most provocative question in his speech, and one of the most important of the entire conference. At its most profound level, no one ever answered it.

• • • • • • • • • • • • • • •

Joaquim Chissano challenged the world's leaders to become geo-partners because he knows that the old paradigm – the rich giving money to the poor – is not the answer. His question – 'What do the poor have to give to the rich?' – was a fitting riddle for global citizens. The purpose of his question was not to be answered, but to awaken.

Any first-year student in economics or political science can explain what the World Bank can give Mozambique. But the question of what Mozambique can give the World Bank requires deeper reflection. Although Chissano's Portuguese-speaking African nation on the edge of the Indian Ocean is far away from the centres of power, his land and his people are part of the solution to the puzzle of building a just and sustainable global civilization. He knows that, without vital geo-partnerships, humankind will lose the game of survival. His challenging question requires that we find a new kind of partnership between the so-called 'haves' and 'have-nots'. If the poor use the same unsustainable strategies to become rich, the world will not survive. In fact, the 'have-nots' possess something the 'haves' need.

Because the poor and the rich share the same world, the choices made by the four billion people in poverty – who are living on less per day than the price of a latte at Starbucks – are the keys to our human future. If the poor become *consumer clones* in the style of the currently affluent, the world will implode. If the poor become *terrorists*, the world will explode. However, if the poor geo-partner with the affluent, humanity has a good chance to find ways to live sanely on this small and precious planet. Human survival depends in great measure on whether we learn to geo-partner: to work together across the boundaries that divide us.

The most respected global leaders understand this. None of them achieved their goals alone. Mandela could not have orchestrated his own freedom, much less the liberation of South Africa, without help. A powerful movement within southern Africa, and supporters all over the world, created the leverage that led to his liberation from prison and his elevation to the presidency. Similarly, without a legion of ministers and their congregations, Martin Luther King, Jr. would have been overwhelmed by the concerted effort to undermine his leadership. The civil-rights movement in the United States gained traction and achieved its goals because it mobilized people of all races and creeds to stand together for human decency.

Even smaller, less historic triumphs required concerted effort by co-leader teams. Arlene Blum was the official leader of the all-women team of climbers that ascended the Himalayan peak Annapurna. But if one observes the extraordinary heroism required for their success, it quickly becomes clear reaching the summit was the result of a team, not just one leader. Similarly, when the Apollo 13 spacecraft was severely damaged and the lives of the astronauts were in danger, Eugene Kranz was the flight director in charge of bringing them safely back to Earth. The achievement was not his alone, but the result of a 'latticework of teams' whose collective, creative synergy pulled life from almost certain death.

When the pieces work together, the whole is strengthened. When geo-partnering happens, new possibilities emerge. This is why global citizens in every part of the world are becoming geo-partners: *nothing else works*. The old, top-down, great-man-giving-orders model of leadership does not flourish in a cross-boundary, global society. Even conventional 'establishment' figures are recognizing that a single nation, no matter how powerful, cannot dictate its will globally. 'There is virtually nothing the United States can do better without others,' observes Richard Haass, President of the Council of Foreign Relations (US). Echoing President Chissano, Haass advises us to 'never forget that foreign policy is forged in a context that all relationships (even between unequals) *must be reciprocal*.'[4]

Sometimes a single, charismatic leader, or a great nation, can make the right decision alone. But far more commonly, unilateral action that does not gain the support of others proves to have been short-sighted, if not plain wrong. Geo-partnering is not a utopian ideal. It is a practical imperative.

● ● ● ● ● ● ● ● ● ● ● ● ● ● ●

🌐 Conference Centre. Bellagio, Italy. 5–9 April 2005.

I was clearly nervous. As I checked into my room, I quickly changed my sweat-stained shirt. To calm myself, I sat down and re-read the description of the meeting I was about to facilitate.

Behind the formal title of this meeting ('Unprecedented Conversations: Broadening Notions of AIDS Treatment and Care for Africa') was an unfolding drama with two sets of protagonists: Western-trained medical doctors with advanced degrees and powerful drugs, and African-trained traditional healers with deep cultural knowledge and potent herbs. The challenge of this meeting was to turn this cross-cultural medical tug of war into a collaboration.

'In Africa, more than in Asia,' wrote Mary Ann Burris, who organized the meeting, 'there has been a struggle between those who favour traditional medicine and those pushing for access to anti-retroviral drugs (ARVs) – and yet, lived experience again and again points us in the direction of recognizing and accommodating both . . . '[5]

Before I reached the meeting room, I encountered one of the African AIDS experts in the hallway. 'Good to meet you,' she said to me, after I introduced myself. 'You're the facilitator, right?'

I nodded.

'A lot of people back home are watching this meeting,' she said. 'I just *pray* it goes well.'

'I hope so too,' I replied. Although I felt like a man stepping off the edge of a cliff into the unknown, I said no more. It served no purpose at this point to burden her with my fears.

As we walked in silence toward the meeting room, I reflected on the conundrum of dealing effectively with HIV/AIDS in Africa.

Everyone attending the meeting was dedicated to bringing the best care for those suffering from this debilitating, frightening disease. The problem was, not everyone agreed on how to do so. Some, particularly those from Europe and America, believed that ARV (anti-retroviral) drugs were the best approach. Designed to inhibit the reproduction of HIV in the body, anti-retroviral medications had been tested and been proven effective in protecting the immune system and delaying the onset of AIDS.

But many of the Africans had strong reservations about Western drugs, which were so expensive that their patients could not afford them. To make matters worse, ARVs often had severe side-effects that poor African communities simply could not handle.

The question was not: which side was right? The question was: could they work together to help the millions suffering from AIDS in Africa?

'What if the Western AIDS activists and the African healers don't listen to each other?' my colleague asked me as we entered the meeting room.

'So many lives depend on them,' I said. 'They must.'

● ● ● ● ● ● ● ● ● ● ● ● ● ● ● ●

When dealing with life-and-death issues such as health care, hunger and malnutrition, war and peace, geo-partnering is a moral imperative. If we think about the urgent global issues that our generation must face, it is abundantly clear that their solution depends on whether we human beings can work together effectively across boundaries. Consider any one of these issues:

- reducing poverty
- sustaining the environment
- peacemaking, conflict prevention, combating terrorism
- replacing water deficits
- strengthening international institutions
- expanding educational opportunities

- defeating global infectious diseases
- preventing and mitigating natural disasters.[6]

Every one of them presents human civilization with the challenge of working effectively across the great social, economic, cultural, and religious divides. *None* of these issues, not a single one, can be resolved by one leader, or one sector of society, or one country, or one organization. Citizens 1.0–3.0 will not succeed; Citizens 4.0–5.0 are absolutely vital.

In this chapter, we will illustrate the capacity of geo-partnering within the context of the first three issues: (1) reducing poverty, (2) sustaining the environment, and (3) building peace. These three have been selected because if we fail badly at any one of them, we ultimately will not succeed at the others.

1. Reducing Poverty

Of the many questions global citizens can ask about poverty, perhaps the most important is: 'What are the rules of the global economic game?' Many people, throughout the world, are sports fans. We watch major global sporting events such as the Olympics or the World Cup, as well as high-visibility national competitions like the National Basketball Association Championships in the United States or the soccer competitions in Brazil, France, Italy, or the UK. No matter how diverse the sports, we observe three common elements: a field, ring, pool, or court with boundaries; rules which are accepted by all sides; and referees who interpret and apply the rules. When the fairness of any of these components is in question, such as in the pairs figure-skating competition at the 2002 Winter Olympics, outrage ensues and the officials become suspect.

Unfortunately, if we shift our focus from global sports to the global economy, the playing field, the rules, and the referees are much less clear. Unlike global athletic competition, the economic 'field' is not always clearly marked or level; the regulations are not agreed to by all sides; and the officials who interpret the rules are not democratically selected or necessarily widely respected. The problem is that more powerful nations have shaped the global rules based on double standards: one for 'us', and another for 'them'. From a Citizen 3.0 perspective, doing so is not only acceptable, but patriotic. But from a Citizen 4.0–5.0 perspective, it is unacceptable, unfair, and ultimately counterproductive.

Unjust rules prevent healthy competition. Instead of a vibrant contest of ideas and approaches, unfair or unclear rules produce bickering, animosity, and ultimately anger and violence. All the rules that govern human life, particularly those implemented by intergovernmental institutions like the International Monetary Fund and the World Trade Organization, have to be viewed through the lens of this question: do they help or hinder those who are affected by them to meet the challenges they face?

'If we are all living on this planet, we should all share responsibility,' says Bharrat Jagdeo, President of the Caribbean nation of Guyana. Jagdeo complains that his nation is told to safeguard its forests by 'the richest nations on Earth', who 'do not honour environmental treaties'. But then these same rich nations, who piously claim that they want to reduce global poverty, turn around and prevent products from poor nations from gaining fair access to global markets. 'We need market access if we are going to become independent and self-reliant,' this young, charismatic President observes. 'All the progressive statements from the head of the World Bank, all these summits – all that does not change that *we feel the system is unfair*.'[7]

Jagdeo is not alone in expressing this concern about the injustice of the global economy. As global citizens, we need to inform ourselves about this issue and take a stand. We do not need advanced degrees in history to know that those in power, with the wealth and political influence to defend their privilege, rarely embrace the powerless as 'geo-partners'. The past century provides ample evidence that genuine partnership between rich and poor, or between privileged and oppressed, almost always requires action.

• • • • • • • • • • • • • • •

🌐 TexacoChevron Oil Terminal, Escravos, Nigeria. July 2002.

One hundred and fifty protesters commandeered a ferry, and ordered the captain to take them to an offshore oil terminal belonging to Chevron. They stormed onto the terminal and took control of the docks, the airfield, and the gas-production facility.

What took the authorities by surprise was not the daring strategy but the identity of the protesters. They were women, mostly in their fifties and sixties, whom people in the region came to call 'the mamas'. They demanded employment for their families and investment in the local community. They were challenging the rules of the global economy.

Armed only with their dignity, these ordinary wives and mothers from six of the nearby villages in the Niger River delta effectively shut down the Escravos terminal, which produces half a million barrels a day, the majority of the company's Nigeria exports. Despite the country's oil wealth, the delta is one of the poorest regions of the country. By shutting down the transportation system, they essentially blockaded the entire facility. When company authorities threatened to have the women removed by force, they responded by threatening to remove their clothes, a gesture which in their culture would have humiliated the company. Finally, the company had no other choice but to listen to their grievances. What they heard was that these women were tired of watching oil revenues stream out of their community to wealthy government officials in Abuja, Nigeria's capital, and to corporate shareholders in communities scattered across faraway Europe and North America. To these village women and their families, the oil brought nothing – not even jobs. Even their husbands and sons could not find work there.

'I give one piece of advice to all women in all countries,' shouted Anunu Uwawah, a leader of the protesters. 'They shouldn't let any company cheat them.'

● ● ● ● ● ● ● ● ● ● ● ● ● ● ●

In this classic case of effective protest, the 'Mamas' shared their message with the entire world before ending their takeover peacefully in a clear, if temporary, victory. Before the protest, the company had simply ignored the letters that these women had sent. After it, the company agreed to give at least two dozen jobs to residents, to build schools and clinics in the villages, and to install electricity and water systems.

Even more important than these material gains, the protesters caused a shift in TexacoChevron's mindset. Because of this shock therapy, the oil-company executives realized they could no longer buy off their critics. 'In the past we basically dealt with things issue to issue, which basically meant paying money,' admitted Dick Filgate, the Canadian executive who acted as the company's top negotiator during the crisis. 'We now have a different philosophy and that is to do more with communities.'[8] In other words, because of the protest, the company was now willing to explore geo-partnering with the communities.

The lesson that these courageous women taught ChevronTexaco was that freedom must be practised, not just preached. By the standards of Western individualism, all of the citizens in the Niger Delta are 'free'. Every Nigerian child, in theory, is free to get an education, free to find work, and free to follow the dream of self-fulfilment. But what these women know is that this wonderful theory, generated by enlightened European philosophers centuries earlier, flourished in countries subsidized by colonialism. While French and British enlightenment thinkers developed their ideas of democracy, and their countrymen transplanted them to North America, a global economic system was being put into place that turned vast regions of the world – including the Nigerian delta – into their economic colonies.

Geo-partnering is the antidote to the poison of this colonial legacy. Such partnerships are not about corporations deciding unilaterally whom to compensate with a 'gift' for what they have taken from a country. They are about corporations witnessing, learning, and connecting with local communities, and deciding together how their combined assets can benefit them both.

* * * * * * * * * * * * * * * *

🌐 Community Centre. Pavathagiri, India. 2002

Two research staff from Solae, a majority-owned subsidiary of the DuPont Company, are sitting with twenty villagers here in Andra Pradesh. Having lived in this village for several months, they are now part of the community and have built a higher level of trust than any other business people. Their project, called Nutrition for Sustainable Development (NfSD), is an effort to create food products that sustain life in this poor community.

Because Solae is a business, they want to sell their product – a soy protein isolate that enhances the nutritional quality of packaged foods. But they are here to do more than create a market. They are trying to co-create a business model with these villagers that will truly serve both their company and the community.

'We do not want to call our company *Solae*,' one of the villagers tells them. 'We want to call it *Solae Samatha*.'

The word 'samatha' in the local language means 'equality', and it reminds the two Solae researchers that the concept of partnership is truly taking root.

'The shift in leadership is from us selling them products, to all of us working together on an equal footing in a way that creates opportunities for everyone,' says Erik Simanis, Co-director of Cornell University's Center for Globally Sustainable Business, who is partnering with Solae in this project. 'There was a lot of scepticism that needed to be overcome. But over the months that the Solae team spent in Pavathagiri, the project team developed a business strategy that improved the nutrition of the village while creating a viable business that brought new income.'[9]

The business revenue comes in three streams. First, it creates packaged foods integrating Solae's soy protein. Second, it launched a community-run catering business that uses its products. Finally, it has developed long-term 'cooking relationships' with women in the village that involve nutrition education and co-creating new dishes.

Obviously if this approach works in Pavathagiri, it could

work throughout India. The payoff to Solae will come when it spins off NfSD into a profitable social enterprise with an expanding market. The benefit to the village will be better nutrition at a better price.

● ● ● ● ● ● ● ● ● ● ● ● ● ● ●

But what, precisely, does geo-partnering mean between the wealthy and the poor?

First of all, *geo-partnering means respecting the interests of all those affected by the decisions.* On both sides of the Atlantic, governments give farmers huge subsidies to grow crops that can be produced much more cheaply in Africa, Latin America, or Asia, which then floods the world market at artificially low prices, undercutting the economies of entire nations. 'This means that an agricultural commodity that could play a real part in poverty alleviation in southern Africa [and other poor regions] does not do so,' argued the development agency Oxfam in a recent report. 'European [and American] consumers are paying to destroy livelihoods in some of the world's poorest countries.'[10]

Of course this is not how leaders who vote for these subsidies view the issue. 'This is for rural America,' said Representative Larry Combest (Republican) of Texas and Chairman of the House Agriculture Committee, defensively, after passing a $180 billion, multiyear subsidy for American farmers. He was dismissing worldwide criticism of the increase in US farm subsidies that depress crop prices in global markets, and effectively push Third World farmers deeper into poverty. Even according to establishment institutions, such as the World Bank and IMF, such subsidies have a reverse 'Robin Hood' effect on the world economy. 'This is pretty galling,' a senior World Bank official said. 'A few American farmers will benefit, but at the expense of a very large number of poor people in developing countries.'[11]

Fortunately, the Obama administration is taking a new tack. The US government is now beginning to recognize that telling farmers in poor countries what to grow in order to get agricultural aid will not work. Instead, the new approach – modelled on the highly effective Global Fund to Fight AIDS, Tuberculosis and Malaria – is to treat poor farmers as aid geo-partners, not aid recipients.[12]

Second, *geo-partnering means recognizing and treating customers, particularly those who are poor, as human beings and community members, not just 'consumers'.* There may indeed be a 'fortune at the bottom of the pyramid', as economist C. K. Prahalad said in his path-finding, controversial book by that title.[13] But to see the bottom of the pyramid only as a market is to dehumanize the people, undermine the communities, and endanger the ecosystems that sustain them. If we keep Chissano's words in mind, we will remember that the four billion people who live on two dollars a day or less are not just a 'market'. They are families; they are communities; they are cultures. They are creative human beings who may also be artisans and craftspeople and labourers and potentially professionals of all kinds.

Geo-partnering between so-called 'haves' and 'have-nots'[14] requires a level of collaboration between corporations and communities that is so unprecedented that it requires a new vocabulary. In the second edition of the 'Bottom of the Pyramid Protocol', a far-reaching inquiry into this question of rich–poor co-leadership, the two business professors who authored the protocol make clear that this vast population needs to be approached based on 'mutual value' and 'co-creation'. These are not terms that normally come out of business schools in the United States – and that's the point.

According to Erik Simanis, the conventional, we-lead-you-follow, we-sell-you-buy approach is 'Bottom of the Pyramid 1.0'. It sees the world's poor as consumers, and nothing more. The corporation's relationship to them is to sell them whatever it can. Simanis is one of the pioneers of 'Bottom of the Pyramid 2.0', which advocates going 'beyond selling to the poor'. In an essay by this title, Simanis and his colleague Stuart Hart develop a powerful paradigm for geo-partnering that, if followed, could empower the poor, extend entrepreneurial capacities, and maintain the environment. But this challenging triple win is achievable only if the corporation and the community become co-creators of an economic future based on mutual values. According to the geo-partnering model, companies must work 'in equal partnership with communities to imagine, launch and grow a sustainable business' and be based on a relationship between buyer and seller that 'creates value for all partners in terms that are important to each'.

Third, geo-partnering means re-valuing the assets of the rich and poor to find what works best for all parties. The poor *do* have assets. They not only have the power of their labour, they also have knowledge, land, culture, history – and more. If we take a closer look at the more creative efforts by global citizens in business to meet the challenge of poverty, we find that they all have a greater respect for the assets of the poor. From the Global Health Initiative (Merck & Co.) and Global Education Initiative (Intel) to the Business Alliance Against Chronic Hunger (Unilever), all are based on the need for the corporation to partner with the community. These private–public initiatives are effective to the degree that they master the art of true geo-partnering.[15]

'Sustainable solutions will only come from building partnerships,' says Richard Clark, Chairman, President, and CEO, Merck
& Co. The goal, he believes, is to use 'the complementary
expertise of all stakeholders'. Michael Treschow, Chairman of
Unilever, concurs that business solutions to hunger and poverty
must be 'sustainable for both the community and the company'.[16]

Although there is always a risk that such statements can
become slick corporate public-relations efforts to improve an
image, there is now clear evidence that many are evolving into
genuine geo-partnerships in action.

• • • • • • • • • • • • • • •

🌐 Manila, the Philippines. January 1972.

The small dirty hand suddenly appeared right in front of my
mouth, blocking the fork with which I was about to take my
first bite of food.

Eager for a change and a return to modernity, I had just
flown to Manila, the capital of the Philippines. Because my
mother, the daughter of a Dutch missionary, had grown up on
the island of Java, I decided after college to visit the world of
her childhood. After spending six intense months living in
Indonesian villages, I was still in culture shock. After the long
flight, I dropped my backpack at a youth hostel (my twenty-
third birthday was only a few days away) and set out for a
late lunch. I found a restaurant open to the sidewalk that
fitted my budget (US$800 for a six-month journey).

Passing a sign that read 'CUSTOMERS ONLY: No beggars
allowed', I sat down at an empty table and ordered a meal
that, when it arrived, I realized would have been sufficient for
three. Riveted on the food in front of me, I was bringing my
first forkful of sautéed vegetables to my mouth when the little

brown hand appeared, thrust directly in the space between the fork and my lips.

It belonged to a young girl, perhaps ten years old. On her hip was her younger brother; he might have been two or three years old, but it was hard to determine. When children have been malnourished from birth, their bodies often look younger – and their eyes older – than they are.

If she had stood back a step and asked for money, I could simply have given her a few coins. But she was leaning against the table, and had literally forced me to lay the fork back down on the plate. I was so shocked that I just stared at her. My first reaction, for which I still feel deep remorse, was to wish they were not there.

But when I finally turned to look at her, into her frightened, hollow, hungry eyes, I saw the eyes of street children around the world. Her eyes beseeched me, saying: 'You, white man – you who have so much more than you need – give me something so my brother and I can live!' As my eyes filled with tears, and my heart opened, I realized that I wanted to feed them.

Noticing the empty chairs on the other side of my table, I motioned for them to sit down and join me. But this noble sentiment came too late for them. Just then the restaurant owner arrived and, speaking to them in Tagalog, pushed them out of the restaurant and back onto the street.

● ● ● ● ● ● ● ● ● ● ● ● ● ● ●

Just as geo-partnering is needed between rich and poor, so it is required between the poor themselves. In Karnataka, a region of India heavily dependent on agriculture and buffeted by collapsing prices for its primary crops, Shree Krishna Padre, a local farmer, knew that he and his neighbours in the region were struggling to stay alive. With a bachelor's degree in science and a lifetime in farming, Shree Padre knew that they had to find new, sustainable ways of caring for the land. The answers, he decided, were not going to come from faraway laboratories or bureaucrats' offices. They would come from the experience of those who knew the land best: the farmers themselves.

'Pen in the Farmer's Hand' was what Shree Padre called his project, which publishes *Adike Patrike*, a farmer-produced and farmer-authored journal. Instead of scientific, research-oriented articles with questionable applicability to the on-the-ground conditions in Karnataka, *Adike Patrike* accepts articles that share practical success stories. In addition to strengthening sustainable agriculture, 'Pen in the Farmer's Hand' also builds literacy and community.[17]

While technological breakthroughs and individual genius will no doubt play a role in solving the riddle of sustainability, the most likely scenario is that locally based global citizens like Shree Padre and his fellow farmers will be centre stage. When it comes to their land and their livelihoods, they must geo-partner not only with each other, but also with the land. The people who can ultimately best care for it are probably not 'experts' from Delhi or London, but rather the people who have lived on it for generations and who are committed to its well-being.[18]

If the poor make smart choices with the resources they have, their incomes increase and they gain access to the basic, elemental benefits of economic development. Taken individually, this process of reducing poverty is sensible and humane. A cell phone to find out where work is available, a road with a bus service to a nearby village, clean running water, adequate nutrition and health care for newborns and their mothers, homes that protect their inhabitants from the elements – who can argue with humanity's desire to have these benefits of life?

What appears to be sensible individually, however, has dangerous implications collectively. Our biosphere is teaching us that the rich cannot continue their current lifestyles – and the poor cannot become rich the way their predecessors did. As each family, one by one, begins purchasing the commodities they feel they need to live better lives, they take a small step out of poverty and toward what is often called the 'middle class'. But the Earth requires humanity to work together in new ways that not only work for our species, but for the fabric of life on which we depend. The biosphere is not structured to support billions of families making the same choices that the rich have made.

2. Sustaining the Environment

Humanity has no more than a decade, according to reliable estimates, to develop a model for economic development different from the consumer-based London–New York–Tokyo model. If we do not change the highly toxic methods for generating wealth in the world, we will destabilize Earth's climate-control systems, dislodge millions of seaside residents, play Russian roulette with weather patterns, and imperil our fragile home.

As global citizens, this leaves us face to face once again with the inescapable planetary puzzle: how can humanity develop economically in a way that is also environmentally sustainable?

● ● ● ● ● ● ● ● ● ● ● ● ● ●

🌐 Conference Center. Colorado. June 2006.

Former Vice-President Al Gore was seated at one end of the circle. The head of the Competitive Enterprise Institute (CEI), who had released the ads attacking Gore's movie *An Inconvenient Truth*, were seated at the other. My colleague William Ury and I, who were facilitating this 'transpartisan' dialogue entitled 'Climate Change and Energy Security', were seated halfway in between them.

The rest of the twenty-four-person circle consisted of a distinguished political microcosm of Americans, all of whom had a stake in the outcome of the debate on 'global warming'. They ranged from the heads of major renewable-energy organizations and environmental groups such as the Sierra Club to the heads of national coal and gas industry associations close to the Bush administration.

By the third and final morning, they had not only begun to speak to each other, but had admitted that they had learned something from the other end of the spectrum. Gore and the 'environmentalists' had learned that their critics had genuine economic concerns about how fighting global warming might impact productivity. CEI and the 'economists' had learned that global warming represents a genuine threat to human civilization.

But as soon as we approached this hard-won patch of common ground, it turned to quicksand.

'We all agree that America has to be part of a global movement to stop global warming,' said one of the participants, the chairman of a major renewable-energy organization. 'But I am afraid that America *can't* be a leader in the world, because we are almost universally despised. Polls prove that America is one of the most hated countries in the world. We're seen as incredibly selfish. We're viewed as plundering the world for our resources. And when we don't get what we want, we bomb countries that don't go along with us! For God's sake, when my children travel abroad now they pretend they're Canadian because they don't want to be targets. We

Americans can't play a leading role in this movement for climate stability because the world has lost its respect for our country.'

For a moment the room was still, as everyone watched the speaker remove his glasses and wipe his eyes that were rimmed with tears. But within a few seconds, the white-haired businessman from the state of Georgia on the other side of the circle, the head of a major energy conglomerate and one of President Bush's most effective fundraisers, raised his hand. I nodded to him and he began to speak slowly, with a strong Southern accent.

'I can't sit here silently and listen to my country be described that way,' he said, quietly at first. 'The America I know and love is *not* the most selfish country in the world. It is, in fact, the most generous. It's done more for humanity than any country in the history of the world. We are beloved by people around the world. People die *every* day to get across our borders to come and live in America. They respect us and admire our way of life.'

He paused, caught his breath, and then added: 'I'm proud to be an American. So are my children. And I will not let my country be criticized so unfairly without speaking up.'

As scores of hands flew into the air, the tension exploded. The two speakers had triggered a subterranean fault line that was dividing the circle like an earthquake can split a town. The energy in the room, which moments ago had been so respectful, was instantaneously charged and polarized. I knew that the hard-won trust that we had built across the partisan barricades was endangered.

● ● ● ● ● ● ● ● ● ● ● ● ● ●

The polarization at that moment in the meeting was an American microcosm of the world's attitudes today about climate change. The 'environment-versus-economy' debate is now occurring in almost every country in the world. The challenge of geo-partnering on the environment is so intense because humanity does not have several generations to figure out how to change our economy to respect the environment. Either it is addressed soon, or the consequences will be irreversible. Unless we change the system of production that is currently spreading throughout the world, the Earth's climate will be even further disturbed. While opinions differ about how quick and how fatal the impact of current production will be on the water, air, soil, and temperature that sustains life, almost all scientists around the world now agree that we have to de-carbonize development or face serious consequences. Between now and 2020, we have to reconfigure the human economic enterprise. The question is: how?

The disheartening fact is that, in our current high-pollution, high-carbon economy, most nations are either remaining poor or becoming environmentally destructive. Where millions are being lifted out of poverty, such as in India and China, the environment is being rapidly destroyed. And where eco-destructive development is not occurring, poverty often continues to trap millions of families.

Global citizens working on this issue are grasping that it requires a global negotiation on an absolutely unprecedented scale. Facing this challenge involves so many institutions in so many countries that the complexity is staggering – and the timeline is extremely short. Even many well-informed citizens still do not grasp this emerging evidence.

'Until I began to work with the challenge of Earth's changing climate change, I just didn't get it,' admits Peter Goldmark, former President of the Rockefeller Foundation and Chairman and CEO

of the *International Herald Tribune*, and now director of the
Environmental Defense Fund's programme on climate change.
Like others who delve into this approaching calamity of global
proportions, Goldmark grasped that climate change is different
from crises that faced previous generations for one very simple
reason: humanity has to deal with it *together* or we will fail.
Everyone is involved. It's not about one country's crisis, like
apartheid in South Africa or racial segregation in the USA or
oppression in Burma. Even Gandhi, in his struggle for Indian
independence, did not have to deal with every major world
capital. But with climate change, every culture, every capital,
almost every profession, is part of the problem or the solution. It
affects *all* of us.'

'On this issue we need more than *passive* agreement,'
Goldmark emphasizes. 'We need *active* consensus. On most
issues, if somebody won't play, you go on without them. But on
this issue, we need buy-in. And so we have to stay at the negotiating table long enough to see everybody's point of view. It's not
enough for the USA and China, for example, to say yes and for
India to say no. *Everybody* has to say yes.'[19]

Everywhere that human beings are addressing climate change,
they face the same challenge of forging geo-partnerships among
stakeholders with different perspectives and different interests. For
example, the organization South*South*North (SSN) was founded to
'place poverty reduction efforts at the center of all climate change
issues'. With offices in Asia, Africa, and Latin America, it is developing pioneering approaches to poverty that also address the
fundamental ecological issues raised by development.[20]

'SSN created a space for a real partnership,' says its Brazilian
co-leader, Thais Corral. 'As our name clearly indicates, we want
the countries of the global South to be able to talk to each other,

not just to the North. We enable exchange between scientists, engineers, policymakers and community leaders to bring together the different streams of knowledge that are each essential and totally interdependent to responding to the climate change challenge.'[21]

Similarly, another organization focused on dealing with climate change, the Consortium on Capacity Building, is also based on geo-partnering strategies. It called itself a consortium because the word literally means 'a group of institutions who agree to work together to accomplish what no one can achieve alone'. Institutes from around the world with acronyms starting with 'C' for 'climate' – CSIRO in Australia, CICERO in Norway, CERED in Vietnam, etc. – have banded together to try to understand and deal with this unprecedented challenge to humankind.

'Brazil, India, China, South Africa – they have to be involved,' says Michael Glantz, the network's coordinator. 'There are different ways to slice the salami, but you need more than one slice. We need to have real partnerships – not the rider-and-the-horse kind, but a partnership of *co-equals*.'[22]

To build that kind of partnership between adversaries is not easy, as illustrated by the meeting with Al Gore. When the meeting was on the verge of dividing into two polarized camps, I stepped between the two men who had just come into conflict and identified the opportunity that they just opened up for all of us.

'Let's take a moment of silence to remember why we came here in the first place,' I said, because I could not imagine any words that could possibly bridge the chasm that separated the two positions. 'After a minute, when we resume our conversation, let's see if we can hold the views of *both* these two thoughtful, caring men in our hearts.'

After a minute that seemed like an eternity, I called on four speakers from different parts of the circle who had raised their hands. Together, their voices were a chorus of the most remarkable wisdom. They reflected on the complexity of the issue, the generosity *and* selfishness of America. Slowly, over the next days and weeks, the 'liberal environmentalists' and the 'conservative economists' created an alliance across the political spectrum that began to work together to deal with the changing climate that will affect us all.

The bitter quarrel in that room reflected humanity's challenge to turn *sustainable development* into a practical way of life. Although this two-word slogan was only recently invented (it was first coined at the World Commission on Environment and Development in 1987),[23] it has penetrated deeply into global policy debates because it captures a fundamental dilemma. It requires an enormous span to cross the chasm that exists between those two words, 'sustainable' and 'development'. The phrase itself challenges us as global citizens to hold both environmental balance and economic opportunity in our hearts at the same time.

Because true global thinking is so rare, this question is often side-stepped. One side of the 'sustainable development' debate typically emphasizes the first word, while the other side emphasizes the second. Even sophisticated environmental statisticians like Bjørn Lomborg, director of the Environmental Assessment Institute in Denmark and author of *The Skeptical Environmentalist*, cannot seem to hold both words in his hands. 'The focus should be on development, not on sustainability,' he asserts. Focusing on sustainability, according to Lomborg, 'ends up prioritizing the future at the expense of the present. This is backward. In contrast, a focus on development helps people today while creating the foundation for an even better tomorrow.'[24]

This is precisely the kind of black-and-white thinking that prevents the synergy implicit in the powerful phrase 'sustainable development'. Both pieces of the puzzle are needed to solve the riddle; each must catalyse new insight in the other. Global citizens need to learn to be advocates for *both* halves of 'sustainable development' by building a bridge that others can cross long, long after we are gone.

● ● ● ● ● ● ● ● ● ● ● ● ● ● ●

🌐 Cape Town, South Africa. April 2002.

As I land at the airport, I am still reading the forty case studies that I have been sent about 'bridging leaders' around the world. Three of the case studies particularly interest me, and I dog-ear the pages: Tessie Fernandez, the director of a woman's foundation in Cebu City in the Philippines, who created a programme for preventing violence against women; Samuel Kalisch, a businessman from Chihuahua, Mexico, who developed a new strategy for reducing poverty in his region; and Father Eliseo Mercado, a Catholic priest who brought Muslims and Christians together on the island of Mindanao to develop greater trust and reduce the chances of further inter-faith violence.

I place the file of case studies aside and review the agenda for the meeting of the Bridging Leadership Task Force, which I am about to co-lead. The Task Force consists of researchers from thirteen countries on four continents who are studying an aspect of leadership that has never before been the focus of such sustained global enquiry. They are researching how leaders successfully solve complex problems across the great divides in their communities.

The initial research shows that the common denominator seems to be a capacity to bridge. These 'bridging leaders' from around the world have all managed to develop 'co-leaders' from all sides. Whatever the divide may be – between men and women, rich and poor, or Muslim and Christian – the bridging leader is able to work with everyone. As isolated leaders, they would fail. As geo-partners, they can succeed.

'The Spanish word *concertacion* captures it best,' one of the members of the Task Force explained to me. From the Latin meaning 'to decide together', this unique word captures the synergy of many people each doing what they do best. It is a holistic approach to action. It transforms the idea of 'leadership' from an individual capacity to a collective one.

● ● ● ● ● ● ● ● ● ● ● ● ● ● ●

Bridging geo-partnerships are so critical today because global problems require that erstwhile adversaries become partners. 'Protect the old growth forests' activists do not know how to manage the major corporations who produce the wood and paper products on which the global economy depends; and the chieftains of that industry cannot by themselves make the necessary radical changes in the way they operate without the principled pressure of the activist community. Similarly, renewable-energy activists are never going to manage the oil, gas, and electrical-power industries, or the banking conglomerates like Citigroup who finance their operations; but the power-brokers in those enterprises are not going to curb the use of fossil fuels or the emission of greenhouses gases rapidly enough to save the Earth's air without listening to, and learning from, their environmental critics.

Neither 'side' needs to convert to the other's way of thinking. Neither needs to 'give in'. The tension between them is the tension of potential synergy. The key is not to waste it on confrontation for its own sake, but to harness it to make the profound and urgent changes required in virtually every sector of the economy.

Because fulfilling the vision of truly sustainable development is still, in Kofi Annan's words, 'beyond the horizon',[25] global citizens are like pilgrims. They are being called into a new world to find an Earth-based economic philosophy and strategy that transcends the mental models of European ideologues such as Adam Smith and Karl Marx, who were writing within the framework of the industrial era. A new form of development that is simultaneously just and sustainable needs to be invented. Although they do not have a final blueprint, global citizens are generating some tantalizing clues about what it will look like. Some of these elements include:

- reducing waste through better design or new technologies. (A Shanghai carpet factory cut its energy consumption by 92 per cent by redesigning its pumping system.)
- developing closed-loop production systems which, like nature herself, turn 'waste' into either natural nutrients or recyclable products. (Atlanta-based Interface Corporation, which makes carpet, is pioneering a 'zero-waste' approach, transforming a high-pollution industry into a low- or no-pollution one.)
- rewriting business plans in ways that take the Earth into account as part of an overall shift from exploitative to 'natural capitalism'.[26]

- eliminating toxic water discharge (Alcoa) or making almost everything in the product line recyclable or reusable (Xerox).[27]
- reducing consumption where there is too much, and sustainably increasing it where there is too little (as advocated by the 'voluntary simplicity' movement).

Is this process happening quickly enough? Will the shifts promoted by these corporate global citizens be deep and enduring enough to keep the ecosystem intact? Can we develop economically and sustain ecologically at the same time?

Yes, we can – but only if we keep the peace.

3. Building Peace

The challenge of sustainable development is daunting, but still possible. We *can* avert climate catastrophe. Most believe that we *can* feed the hungry, even with some population growth. Most believe that we *can* honour the ecology of the Earth and the needs of humanity. But all this is possible only if we bring our best to the challenge, and if we marshal our resources to do so. If we waste precious human, technological, and natural resources on war, all bets are off.

Why? Because there is no greater destructive impact on sustainable development than humanity's military enterprise.[28]

While governments from around the world are meeting repeatedly in places like Bali and Copenhagen to protect planet Earth from the threat of calamitous climate change, the main 'climate criminal' remains at large. The world's military forces, for example, are responsible for an estimated two-thirds of key chlorofluorocarbons that deplete the ozone layer and endanger human beings. Similarly, while caring government officials convene frequently to develop new strategies for scraping together the necessary funds to achieve the UN Millennium Development Goals in order to lift hundreds of millions out of poverty, the primary wasted expenditure continues unchecked. As of this writing, for example, the costs of the wars in Iraq and in Afghanistan are $666 billion and $187 billion respectively.[29] Similarly, the costs of other hostilities, including the India–Pakistan and the Israel–Palestine conflict, continue to soar.[30]

The truth is: even though negotiation and diplomacy are usually more effective than military action, investment patterns are precisely the opposite. The entire UN Peacekeeping budget is less than 1 per cent of the world's military expenditure – and less than three weeks of US government spending in Iraq. If our species does not invest more in sustainable development and less in war, we will not achieve either development or sustainability.

● ● ● ● ● ● ● ● ● ● ● ● ● ● ●

🌐 Newstands and Front Porches. Washington, DC. 19 May 2009.

'US–Russian Team Deems Missile Shield In Europe Ineffective,' trumpeted the *Washington Post* in a headline that streamed across the top of the page.[31]

The research on which the article was based, released by the EastWest Institute (EWI), had just performed three small miracles. First, it had helped reduce the chances that the US would go to war with Iran. Second, it had improved the relationship between Russia and the US, which following the clash with Georgia had turned increasingly bitter. Third, and equally important, it had given the Obama administration precisely the information that it needed to say no to the Bush administration's plans to start a new arms race in Europe.

How could one report, issued by a largely unknown think-tank, accomplish all this?

The answer, in a word, is geo-partnership.

If six Americans had written this report by themselves, they might have been dismissed as partisan. If six Russian scientists had asserted that the US missile shield was worthless, it would have been dismissed as Kremlin-inspired propaganda. But EWI employed a challenging and ultimately effective cross-boundary strategy of bringing together six Russian and six American scientists over several months to carefully study together the scientific data about whether Iran had the capacity to launch missiles that could strike Europe. The unprecedented composition of this twelve-person, bilateral team enabled them to produce research that had a direct and immediate policy impact not only in Moscow and Washington, but in Tehran and Jerusalem as well.

'The report established that there is no intercontinental Iranian nuclear threat now,' announced EWI President John Mroz. 'The scientists have taken this issue out of the realm of politics, ideology and guesswork, and brought it down to reality.'

• • • • • • • • • • • • • • • •

Whatever issues concern us as global citizens – preventing more war in Afghanistan and Iraq, keeping Pakistani nuclear weapons out of terrorists' hands, stabilizing climate change by reducing carbon emissions, preparing for the coming water crisis – the lessons of humanity's successful collaborations must be remembered. In almost every intractable conflict, global problem-solving depends on partnership. Without a partnership, one 'side' tries to fix the problem but often only makes the problem worse. With a partnership, the two or more 'sides' can come together and design an innovation – something new that did not exist before. For example:

- The United States and its NATO allies cannot win the war in either Afghanistan or Iraq. They need to geo-partner with the citizens in those countries, and their neighbours.
- The US by itself cannot prevent Pakistan from collapsing or secure its nuclear materials. It needs to geo-partner with the Pakistanis to rebuild their country on a firm foundation.
- No single nation can deal with climate change. A consortium of nations must forge a partnership around a set of ecological and economic principles that revolutionize production and consumption around the world.
- No single country, and no single profession, can deal with the coming water crisis. It will require the collective genius of many cultures, and many professions, to discover the efficiencies that will keep the supplies in balance on this planet.

These cross-boundary geo-partnerships do not emerge by magic. They are based on building trust between partners who often have not worked together before, and who initially approach each other with uncertainty, suspicion, and unfounded stereotypes. The process of building trust takes all the skills of global citizenship: to witness the world rather than taking sides; to unlearn stereotypes and discover common ground; and to connect with others across linguistic, cultural, religious, and other divides.

• • • • • • • • • • • • • •

🌐 Downtown Cafe. Nairobi, Kenya. March 2009.

Stella Sabiiti is talking to me about the many violent conflicts that she and her colleagues in the Peace and Security Department of the African Union must somehow keep in check. I feel stunned by both the number and the scale of the problems they face. Kenya had just emerged from a near-genocide only a year before, and we could still feel the shock and fear that had gripped this capital city.

'Darfur . . . the Congo . . . Zimbabwe,' I say slowly, listing the conflicts Stella and her colleagues are confronting. 'How do you deal with all of these violent crises?'

As she begins to reply, her eyes sparkle. Feeling the brightness of the light that shines inside her, I understand why she is known throughout Africa and Europe as one of the most effective and charismatic teachers about conflict transformation.

'When we walk into a violent conflict situation,' she says, 'everything often looks hopeless. It is true. But then – when we take a closer look – we always find that there are islands of peace. There are always people and places who are resilient, who have kept faith with themselves, who have set their eyes on the future they want to build.'

She takes a drink of water, perhaps expecting me to speak. But I sense she has more to say.

'So we are not starting from scratch,' she continues. 'We have natural allies. Our job is to partner with these islands of peace. And when we do . . .' Her beautiful smile completes her sentence. And in the silence that follows, I realize that she has inspired hope in me too.

• • • • • • • • • • • • • •

Ethnic violence erupted in Kenya in late 2007, following a disputed election in which the leader of one tribe allegedly 'stole' the election from a candidate from another tribe. It swept across the nation leading to more than fifteen hundred deaths. It culminated in the appalling murder of fifty people, mostly women and children, in the small Rift Valley town of Eldoret. Trying to protect themselves from a horde of attackers armed with machetes, they locked themselves in the church. But instead, the angry mob burned them alive. Once this cauldron of violence exploded, why didn't the entire country go up in flames? What stopped it?

Nairobi has been called the 'Geneva of Africa' because, like its Swiss namesake, it has been an island of relative tranquillity in a continent filled with violence and war. So the shock waves shook the entire continent. 'Maybe in Burundi or Rwanda,' said one UN official, 'but I never thought this could happen in Kenya.'[32]

Instead of descending into all-out genocide, however, an uneasy and fragile peace took hold. Newspapers around the world showed images of former UN Secretary-General Kofi Annan, who met the leaders of the rival parties and guided them into a power-sharing arrangement. But what truly brought the killing in the villages to an end was a remarkable partnership between two veteran conflict-resolution specialists and – believe it or not – two generals.

Several years earlier, General Daniel Opande had led a UN peace force in Liberia in the midst of its civil war. He saw village after village destroyed and hundreds of innocent civilians massacred. 'It makes me, as an African, feel very sad,' Opande said after viewing one particular brutal attack. 'Because instead of building, we are destroying, and we continue to destroy, and destroy and destroy.'[33]

The other general was Lazaro Sumbeiywo, former Chief of Staff of the Kenyan army. After spending most of his illustrious career making war, he found himself appointed chief mediator of Africa's longest civil war, an intractable and devastating north–south conflict in the Sudan which taught him some unforgettable peace-building skills.[34]

These two generals teamed up with two civil society peace-makers in Kenya, a gifted Muslim mediator named Dekha Ibrahim and a founder of the Nairobi Peace Initiative, George Wachira. Together this unlikely quartet – each from a different tribal background, each with a different constituency and history – orchestrated a much larger team that, working together from their makeshift headquarters in a local hotel, helped bring an end to the violence. Through round-the-clock meetings with scores of civic organizations, by building peace committees in every 'hot' district, the team turned the tide. Instead of Kenya escalating into a full-scale genocide, an uneasy calm took hold that has given the country a chance to heal, to identify the underlying cause of the unrest, and to begin the urgent search for alternatives to violence.

'We would not have succeeded without our entire team,' recalls Ms Ibrahim. 'Every one of us played a vital part. It was a genuine partnership for peace.'

The lesson global citizens can draw from how Kenya narrowly averted a protracted and devastating genocide is that partnerships that cross social divides are essential in peacemaking. Don't take my word for it – go meet the peacemakers yourself. To meet Dekha Ibrahim and other Kenyan peacemakers, simply go to Youtube and enter http://vimeo.com/6519499. Listen to their story and you will hear the words of today's *real* heroes, the global citizens who have the courage and wisdom to transform violence into understanding, and war into peace.

● ● ● ● ● ● ● ● ● ● ● ● ● ●

🌐 Worldwide Security Conference. Brussels, Belgium. February 2009.

Tall, confident, speaking with the authority of a senior statesman, the youthful Afghan chairing the panel addresses the room of Western security specialists about his country. I listen with rapt attention, eager to hear the perspective of a citizen of Afghanistan. After months of listening to American politicians and NATO officials, it is refreshing – at long last – to listen to the voice of an Afghan speaking his mind about what his country wants.

The speaker is Hekmat Karzai, the Director of the Centre of Conflict and Peace Studies in Kabul, and a cousin of President Hamid Karzai. Unless the West wants to get bogged down in an endless war, Hekmat advised that the West 'listen far more intently . . . Tribal leaders and elders must be invited to give their leadership about how best to proceed in Afghanistan . . . what works and what does not.' In addition to speaking eloquently about the possible partnership between outside forces and Afghan leaders, Hekmat bluntly shared fundamental facts about which outsiders remain unaware. 'Do you know,' he asked, 'that the Taliban pay their forces three times as much as the Afghan National Army pay theirs?'[35]

Hekmat was far more persuasive than any of the outsiders who spoke about his country. I wondered how long it would be before the military top brass started listening to Afghans like Hekmat, and working with them as true partners.

● ● ● ● ● ● ● ● ● ● ● ● ● ●

Imagine that you live in a country that is being 'freed' by the army of a foreign power. Year after year, from planes that fly so high that you can barely see them, bombs fall on villages near where you live. The foreign officials claim they are attempting to kill the people who are oppressing you. But again and again, it is innocent civilians who are killed. When your country protests and seeks to hold them accountable for their inhuman actions, they deny or minimize the number of deaths. How long would you continue wanting to be 'freed' by such an army?

In November 2008, a United States Air Force AC-130 gunship mistook a wedding of a tribal leader for a Taliban gathering and killed dozens of innocent civilians. Afghans were outraged by the denials and lies coming from the occupying forces. Even President Karzai complained that it was hard to win over the 'hearts and minds' of the Afghan people when bombs rained down on women and children. Against the backdrop of the tragedy, Kai Eide, the Norwegian chief of the UN mission in Afghanistan, held a press conference. In order not to criticize the US military directly, he posed a series of questions: 'Are we sufficiently sensitive to Afghan concerns? Are we sure that we are behaving in a way that brings Afghan communities closer to the government? Do we listen sufficiently to the concerns we hear from the President and so many Afghans?' He paused, and then added: 'We see how we can go wrong now.'[36]

Six months later, however, another US bombing raid killed more than a hundred innocents in the western village of Granai. Again, the same pattern repeated itself: human rights organizations said a hundred and seventeen civilians were killed (including sixty-one children and twenty-six women), while US military officials discounted the claims as Taliban propaganda. Finally, one month later, the US commander in Afghanistan, Lieutenant-General Stanley McChrystal, acknowledged that American military personnel made 'significant errors' and admitted that military progress would ultimately be 'hollow and unsustainable' unless attacks on civilians were stopped.[37]

Incidents such as these, which have continued unabated throughout the war in Afghanistan, demonstrate the impossibility of winning a war without geo-partnering. Unfortunately, it has taken the US military far too long to learn that 'winning the war' is not a strictly military matter but requires genuine collaboration with the Afghan people.

When the US Army finally decided to hire skilled anthropologists and assign them to combat units in Afghanistan and Iraq, the results were remarkable. After the arrival of the anthropologists, said Colonel Martin Schweitzer, commander of the 82nd Airborne Division, the unit's combat operations were reduced by 60 per cent. As a result, his troops were able to focus on improving overall security, health care, and education. Instead of being locked in battle 'focused on the enemy', said Schweitzer, 'we're focused on bringing governance down to the people.'[38] Wherever anthropologists were assigned and their counsel followed, results were consistently positive. Other American military officials, who called the social scientists' advice 'brilliant', concluded that anthropologists increased the military's ability to view the situation through Afghan eyes and decreased the need for combat operations.[39] In other words, when the military evolved from Citizen 2.0 to 3.0 to 4.0, they became far more effective.

'We mistakenly think that the richest country in the world with the biggest intelligence apparatus and the greatest access to information knows more than anyone else,' says Dr Hugh Gusterson, a professor of anthropology at George Mason University. 'But in fact, the ones who understand the world the least are often the most privileged. The attitude of the military is that if we just use more power and more of the weapons in our military arsenal, we will win. They persist in thinking that, if we simply try harder and "stay the course", we will remove al-Qa'eda from Pakistan, end the insurgency in Afghanistan and bring harmony to Iraq. We anthropologists know they are wrong – but they do not want to hear that from us.'[40]

A similar illusion has dogged the war in Afghanistan. Foreign troops are failing to bring peace. But that should not surprise us, since three times that number of Soviet troops met with complete failure a generation ago. Like the Soviets, other invaders ranging from Alexander the Great to the British also failed to dominate the region. Yet Western military leaders and politicians continue to propose the same ill-fated proposal: more troops.

'If we were to have the same density of soldier per square kilometre as in Kosovo,' observes German diplomat Ortwin Hennig, who was posted in Kabul for many years, 'NATO would need to deploy another 300–400,000 troops – *which is out of the question*. NATO's approach is too militarized; we need to demilitarize our strategy.'[41]

In all fairness, the compelling counter-argument of the die-hard militarists is that one cannot 'geo-partner' with the ideological fanatics and ruthless killers that join al-Qa'eda and its Taliban supporters. In one sense, I believe they are right: hate-filled zealots committed to violence and unwilling to change must be stopped by military means. However, US intelligence operatives consider that only ten per cent of Taliban fighters fit this description. According to David Kilcullen, Senior Counterinsurgency Adviser, Multi-National Force – Iraq, who served on the personal staff of US Army General David Petraeus, no more than one out of ten Taliban are die-hard terrorists. With the proper incentives, Kilcullen believes, the other ninety per cent would lay down their arms and participate in the rebuilding of Afghan society.[42]

If we need further evidence that geo-partnering can work in the Middle East, journalist Daniel Gavron has provided it. Through his detailed interviews with scores of Palestinians and Israelis who are working together in every conceivable way – as educators, doctors, farmers, human-rights activists, and neighbours – he has demonstrated that geo-partnering is possible even in the most intense, embittered war zones. Although Gavron realizes that the Israeli–Palestinian conflict 'remains grave and deadlocked', he has witnessed with his own eyes that 'it does not have to be so. Thousands of people in hundreds of projects are proving this every day.' He concludes that, despite the ongoing violence and hatred, Jews and Arabs can coexist, as proved by the fact that some of them do so every day.[43]

One of these Middle Eastern geo-partners, Shlomo Hasson, is no stranger to the injustices of his region. As a boy Hasson watched his family lose their home in Hebron in 1929 during an Arab pogrom. But instead of fuelling hatred and revenge in him, it generated a commitment to geo-partnering with Palestinians who are now experiencing the same suffering that he did.

'The first step is recognition of the Other, the plight of the Other, the suffering of the Other,' says Hasson, a professor at the Hebrew University. 'Whenever I think of the Palestinians, inside or outside Israel, I am aware of the historic injustice. We as Jews tend to justify our position out of insecurity. We need to find the inner security to be able to listen to their suffering and to respond to it.'[44]

During a board meeting of the New Israel Fund several years ago, Hasson took his colleagues to a promontory overlooking the heart of Jerusalem. 'When you look at the city at night, you can tell where the Jewish settlement and the Palestinian set-tlements are located,' he said, as he waved his arms toward the holy sites in the Old City. 'The minarets of the mosques are illu-minated with a ring of green neon. The watchtowers of Israeli security are illuminated with blue neon. What you will notice is that, almost everywhere, the two colours are intertwined. It is not two separate worlds, but a patchwork. In this country, you can divide almost anything . . . but not Jerusalem.'[45]

To transform the current enmity into such synergy, Hasson knows that extraordinary and courageous partnerships between Palestinians and Israelis will be needed – not the petty, bitter wrangling of politicians, but the courage and compassion of both Arabs and Jews who are able, and willing, to lead beyond borders. Their partnerships – based on the skills of witnessing, learning, and connecting – will one day be the buildings blocks of a lasting peace.

Such geo-partnerships are how we can reduce poverty, how we can respect the environment, and how we can keep the peace. Every one of us can be such a partner. All we have to do is to reach out to someone else who shares our concerns and work together. Thousands of global citizens are already 'bridging the global gap', 'working together across boundaries and against the odds to forge extraordinary geo-partnerships'.[46] They do not make excuses for why they cannot make a difference. Instead, however challenging their circumstances may be, they find the resources to act.

'Somehow the money that came into the country to support development always ended up in the hands of men,' recalls Virginia Mupanduki, who is from Zimbabwe. Troubled by the systematic exclusion of women in her country, she attended a conference in Cairo on the Role of Women in Rural Development, where she learned that the problem she faced is a worldwide scandal. Even though at the time she could barely read and write, she found the courage to speak up at the conference and explain to the other delegates the problems she and her fellow country-women faced.

Encouraged by the reactions of the other women there, and by concrete support from funding organizations, she returned to Zimbabwe determined to create opportunity for women. The result was the Zimbabwe Adult Learners Associations, a network of organizations that is now enabling women throughout the country to become educated, start small businesses, and become active in civic life.

Virginia Mupanduki's story is inspiring because, when she noticed that 'men' were the problem, she didn't wait for them to change. Instead of just exhorting men to start treating women fairly, she formed a geo-partnership that catalysed a transformation in herself and in her country.

Whether you and I happen to be a woman or a man, young or old, rich or poor, we can reach out to someone who shares our concerns and work together.

Global Intelligence: Twenty Ways to Raise Our GI

*We cannot solve problems on the same level of
awareness that we created them.*

— **Albert Einstein**

Developing the four capacities outlined in this book – witnessing, learning, connecting, and geo-partnering – will raise our 'global intelligence'. Unlike IQ, which is our intelligence quotient, or our EQ, which is our emotional quotient, GI is our ability to use all our faculties in ways that cross the borders that separate humankind. If we crystallize the extensive research on this subject, the most succinct and straightforward definition of global intelligence is: the human capacities that enable us to coexist and co-create with people different than ourselves.

GI involves all of who we are, not just our intellects. It may trigger every human emotion, ranging from the excitement of discovering our connections to each other to the despair of learning about inequality and injustice; from the delight of travelling to distant lands to the confusion of more complexity than we can digest. Becoming global citizens may fill our hearts with emotions that we might otherwise rarely know. It is not just about how we think, but also how we feel; not just about what we know, but how we act.

Among the many tests that measure our GI, one of the most sophisticated is the 'global mindset' inventory, based on the pioneering work of Professor Mansour Javidan and his colleagues at the Thunderbird School of Global Management.[1] I encourage you to take this (or another similar) skills inventory to assess your current GI.

However, continuing to develop our GI throughout our lives is ultimately more important than our 'score' on a test at one point in time. What matters is discovering daily, lifelong activities for consciously developing your global intelligence that work best for you. After all, 'raising your GI and becoming a global citizen' is not a college course that lasts a semester, but rather a journey that lasts a lifetime.

Gathered from many sources, as well as my own experience conducting global leadership training around the world, here are twenty daily ways to stimulate global intelligence. Because they raise our GI, they will also help us deal with an increasingly complex and challenging world. Please do not use them as mere brain-teasers, but rather as ways to fashion a globally aware life. Whether you focus on a few of them, or pursue them all, please weave them into the fabric of your life. Doing so will help you find your own unique path to global citizenship – enriching your life *and* making a better, safer world.

NOTE: The Global Citizens' Resources section that follows this chapter contains specific books, websites, organizations and other tools for exploring each of these GI-raising methods.

1. Be the change that you want to see in the world.

Gandhi's oft-quoted advice is the right starting point for us because, if followed, it challenges us to go inward and go outward at the same time. It encourages us not to wait for 'them' to change, but to change ourselves first.

In this spirit, I must admit that the biggest obstacle to my achieving change in the world has been me. Although I have been fortunate to have many opportunities to contribute to the world during my life, I have missed some of them because I was not then aware of the parts of myself that were part of the problem. I was so determined to be a 'caring' person, and ultimately a 'global' citizen, that I remained blind to the parts of myself that were not caring and not global. I was so determined to be generous, for example, that I did not recognize how I was selfish;

and so committed to being collaborative that I did not admit when I was headstrong, etc.

For me, following Gandhi's advice has been highly practical as well as spiritual counsel. When he encouraged us to 'be the change that [we] want to see in the world', he was not advocating personal instead of socio-political change but rather internal change as a means to achieving external change. This distinction in interpretation is crucial if we are to become global citizens who walk in his footsteps.

The profiles of global citizens in this book are evidence that the key is to start with who we are, and where we are. We met global citizens with great power and influence, like UN diplomats, and those who have very little influence or wealth, like Zimbabwean Virginia Mupanduki. But no matter which global citizen we met – from Israeli and Palestinian peace-builders to African healers, from astronauts returning from orbit to university students in Zhuhai – the starting point for all of us is the same: here, and now.

If we want a compassionate, caring world, let us be compassionate and caring for those around us. If we want a just world, let us live justly. If we want a sustainable world, let us create lives that are sustainable. If we want a peaceful world, let us be peace.

2. Use both sides of your brain.

Brain research has recently established that our minds tend to filter out information that challenges our identities. When we listen to speeches by public figures that include statements with which we disagree, our brains 'turn off'; when they make statements that confirm what we already believe, our brains 'turn on'.

If, for example, a Muslim sympathetic to al-Qa'eda heard a

speech by a US Army general in Iraq, he would immediately discount whatever he heard, even if it were true. An American television viewer who heard a speech by Osama bin Laden would do exactly the same. Our left brain performs this screening function in order to protect our identity. The goods news is that by filtering out information that does not fit our current worldview it gives us a cushion of certainty. But the bad news is: it prevents us from learning.

Fortunately, our brain has two hemispheres. In simple terms, the left brain thinks, the right brain feels.[2] We need to use both of them to raise our global intelligence. When our left brain 'shuts down' in the face of challenging evidence, our right brain can feel us contract and tighten. It can alert us to the fact that we are being 'closed-minded'. It can challenge us to show more respect (literally, to 'look again'). It can remind us to open our minds and to listen deeply to (not necessarily agree with) even points of view that strike us as outrageous, misinformed, and even immoral.

The *corpus callosum* is the vital part of the brain that connects the left and the right hemispheres. This 'switchboard' brings the skills of both parts of the brain together. Although it tends to be more highly developed in women than in men, every one of us can develop it more fully by becoming more familiar with its function and using it to keep the door of our minds open to the world.

Recently the GLOBE project, the multi-country research initiative that developed the concept of the 'global mindset', hired two neuroscientists to begin studying the differences in brain function between those who were global thinkers and those who were not. Using electrodes connected to an EEG, they found that many sectors on both sides of the brain would 'fire' simultaneously in subjects with high GI, while those with lower GI would function almost entirely in one region on the left side of the brain. While this research is still too preliminary to be conclusive, the early results suggest that whole brains are much better at witnessing the world than only a part.[3]

Note to parents: although television can build GI, please keep it out of the bedrooms of young children. The development of television has clearly strengthened the global part of ourselves insofar as it brings us news about communities and cultures other than our own. However, television in the bedrooms of young children is quite another matter. Children with televisions in the room where they sleep score lower on school tests and develop other negative behaviour patterns. The risks of television in children's bedrooms outweigh whatever the benefits may be.[4]

3. Remember that 'one' comes before 'two'.

In September 2008, more than a hundred Muslim scholars and clerics of all sects wrote an open letter to the world's Christians that should be required reading. From across the Muslim world, they reached out to remind their Christian brethren that Osama bin Laden does *not* represent them. They pointed out how much Islam and Christianity share, including belief in the unity of God, the primacy of love for God, the power of loving thy neighbour, etc. Their letter, entitled 'A common word between us and you', catalysed a response from many Christians, including the Archbishop of Canterbury, who concluded his reply with these words: 'So to your invitation to enter deeply into dialogue . . . we say: *Yes! Amen.*'[5]

Raising our GI means keeping our eye on what we share, not only on what we don't. Yes, our faiths differ – but developing our global intelligence quickly reveals that our faiths also share common ground. Despite the tensions between the so-called 'Christian West' and the 'Muslim Middle East', both these faiths, as well as Judaism, began in one family – the family of Abraham.

Readers of this book may be Muslim or Hindu, Jewish or Christian. The people who hold this book in their hands may be Arab or Caucasian, Swiss or Swazi. On the one hand, becoming a global citizen means exercising what Jason Hill, a young Jamaican-born philosopher, calls 'the right to forget where you came from'.[6] It means uprooting ourselves from our historical identities. But on the other hand, raising your GI does not mean turning away from your roots, but turning into them.

Whatever our identities are, if we trace them deeper and deeper, they will take us into the oneness of the Earth. 'Read the Bible, read the Koran, read the Torah, the Upanishads, the *Bhagavad Gita*,' said the late Indian guru Swami Satchidananda, in one of his clearest and most succinct statements. '[All faiths] say . . . Get out of these definitions. It's the definitions that divide us.'

Wherever we dare to look beneath the surface differences we find an unexplored or undeveloped oneness. Before we split into many, we were one. To remember this simple but elusive truth, a simple exercise is this: whenever you say, 'One, two, three,' remember that one comes first.

4. Make sure your house has a door.

As everyone knows, a house needs a door. Otherwise it is no longer a home, but a prison. But when it comes to religion, we often build houses of worship without doors. We create belief systems with walls but no exits.

All over the world fundamentalist parents of every faith believe that it is bad for children to learn about other ways of seeing the world, particularly ways that they consider evil. In the United States, for example, there are millions of followers of Jesus Christ who mistrust anyone who follows Mohammed and who would never encourage their children to study the Koran or read about Islam. Halfway around the world, in the thousands of fundamentalist religious schools called *madrasas* from Morocco to Mindanao, there are hundreds of millions of followers of the prophet Mohammed who do not want their children to study the Bible or read about Christianity. And scattered throughout the world are Jews, who live as a minority among the other Abrahamic faiths, and who inculcate their children into Judaism.

Of course parents of all faiths have the right to give their children a religious 'home' in order to ensure that they adopt the same faith as their parents. Although ignorance about one's neighbours is not good for anyone, parents around the world teach their children about their own traditions and very little, if at all, about the faiths of others.

However, when we live in a community, we should know enough about our neighbours to be able to respect their way of life (and they should know us sufficiently to respect ours). After all, we global citizens are not only members of our respective religions; we are also stewards of Creation, which includes people of all faiths. The more we know about Creation and all its creatures, including the two-legged, the better we can take care of it – and ourselves.

5. Think like a minority.

At home in Colorado, where I live with my family and spend time with local friends, it is easy for me as a 'white man' to believe that I am in a racial and ethnic majority. After all, most of the people around me day to day look like me. But if I drive a few hours south, I will be in towns where seven out of ten people are Hispanic, or nine out of ten Native American. If I fly to Mexico City, or to Beijing, I become part of a minuscule white minority. To become global citizens, we need to remind ourselves of this fundamental truth: every one of us is a member of a minority.

To underscore this point, imagine for a moment that you are a member of the largest ethnic group in the world, the Han Chinese. They constitute approximately 92 per cent of the total population of the People's Republic of China. Although this means that there are more than one billion Han Chinese, they are still less than 20 per cent of the total human population. In other words, even the Han Chinese are a minority of humanity.[7]

So whatever the colour of our skin or the shape of our face, and regardless whether our neighbours resemble us or not, it is important for us to think like a member of a minority simply because we are one. This awareness makes us more mindful that we are only one patch in the quilt of humanity, only one of many kinds of leaves in the forest. Ethnically speaking, we are not the rule, but the exception.

6. Increase your knowledge – including how to not-know.

'What should every global citizen know?'

I will never forget what happened when I posed this very direct question to a group of twenty thoughtful colleagues gathered at a global conference. As soon as I asked it, this distinguished group offered their rapid-fire replies.

'Ecological literacy,' said Fritjof Capra, author of *The Tao of Physics* and *The Web of Life*.

'Sustainable economics,' said Hunter Lovins, one of the co-authors of *Natural Capitalism*.

'Understanding financial systems,' said Jeff Gates, an economist.

'Systems thinking,' said a professor from a leading university.

'Physics and biology,' said another participant.

'World religions,' said a more spiritually oriented colleague.

As the list of 'must-learn' subjects continued to grow, the mood in the room shifted from excitement to confusion. The avalanche of answers almost buried us alive. In less than five minutes, they had outlined a curriculum equal to half a dozen graduate degrees!

I share this experience because 'keep learning' is paradoxical. At first it can be empowering; but ultimately, it is not enough since no one can know it all. Yet many gurus of global thinking seem to be unaware of the left brain's limitations. For example, Jeffrey Sachs, Director of Columbia University's Earth Institute, advises us to become global citizens by learning about 'this generation's challenges' by 'studying development economics, climate change, public health, and other relevant fields'. (He adds that *Nature, Science, New Scientist, Discover*, and *Scientific American* are 'must-reads for our age', and then encourages us to stay abreast of 'countless high-quality Web sites' as well.)

While I have the greatest respect for this gifted economist, certainly one of the most effective global citizens at work in the world today, I must disagree with his advice. His research assignment is so daunting (and requires so much leisure time) that I doubt most human beings – even his full-time graduate students – would be able to follow it.

Which is why I suggest instead: keep learning – including how to not-know.

'Not-knowing does not mean you don't know,' said Zen master Suzuki Roshi, who developed the concept of 'beginner's mind'. On the contrary, it means not being *attached* to what we know, and being able to hold our knowledge lightly. It means being able to think beyond the limits of the known. So a vital part of cross-boundary learning is becoming aware of what we do not know. Not-knowing is a key to becoming global citizens because it will keep us steady, confident, and humble in a world of infinitely expanding information.

7. Test your worldview against the actual facts.

Q. What country has the largest number of Muslim citizens?
A. India B. Saudi Arabia C. Indonesia D. Egypt.

As you reflect on your answer, take a moment to reflect on your state of mind. Are you sure about your answer? If so, do you remember how you first learned about the Muslim faith (or religions other than your own)? What shaped your image of these 1.3 billion people? And is your image based on first-hand experience, or second-hand information?

The correct answer is '(C). Indonesia'. (The nation with the second largest Muslim population, by the way, is India.) As this suggests, the vast majority of Muslims live in Asia, not the Middle East. If you answered that question correctly, congratulations! You have freed yourself from the mass media stereotype that most Muslims are Arabs (in fact, only 20 per cent are). You have an accurate sense of the geographical and cultural distribution of this vast and diverse religious community. If your answer was incorrect, take it as an opportunity to learn.

Here's another more controversial question on which to test your worldview:

> Q. Which economy catalysed the recovery from the most recent global recession?
>
> A. The United States B. China C. Europe Union D. Russia.

In previous eras, the right answer would have been 'A. The United States'. Typically, previous global economic slumps were turned around by American economic enterprise. The USA would spur growth, and Europe would follow close behind. But the 2008 recession was different. The United States did not lead the pack, but followed it. This time the hero of the story was in Asia. 'The economic centre of gravity has been shifting for some time, but this recession marks a turning point,' said Neal Soss, chief economist for Credit Suisse. 'It's Asia that's limiting the world, rather than the US, and that's never happened before.' Jeffrey Garten, former Undersecretary of Commerce for International Trade in the Clinton administration, agreed: the 'locomotive for global recovery' will not be the US; it will 'have to be China, where growth is humming along . . . '[8]

Yes, 'B. China' is the correct answer. 'Asia's Recovery Highlights China's Ascendancy' happened to be the banner headline in the business section of the *New York Times*, but the same story was reported in the *Financial Times*, *The Economist*, and other publications.[9] It was Asia, followed by the European Union, that emerged first from the recession. The USA came later.

As the question suggests, raising your GI means letting real experience challenge your 'mental map' of the world and continuing to renew and revise your worldview as long as your heart beats.

8. Know your enemy – inside and out.

On the eve of the Iraq war, an American columnist wrote: 'The question before us is very large and very simple: "Can – and will – the *civilized* part of humanity disarm the *barbarians* who would use the ultimate knowledge for the ultimate destruction?" '[10] This kind of language is not useful if we are truly going to 'know our enemies'. In fact, it does just the opposite: it makes us 'civilized' (i.e. human) and them 'barbaric' (i.e. subhuman). This simplistic dualism leads not only to ineffective political strategy, but also to inept military action.

'Knowing your enemy' is not an idealistic, save-the-world notion, but rather a practical, hard-headed way to use our GI in order to keep ourselves, and our loved ones, safe.

Although the biblical advice to 'know your enemy' is thousands of years old, we human beings have unfortunately not followed it very well. Even though every faith, in one form or another, admonishes its followers to 'do unto others as you would have others do unto you', we have tended to do so only when the 'others' are like us. When the 'others' are very different from us, we have often conveniently forgotten this golden rule.

If we want to bequeath to our children a more secure world, empathizing with our adversaries, actual or potential, is essential. According to veteran national security officials like Zbigniew Brzezinski, we all too often deal with enemies, particularly those we call 'terrorists', as if they were 'suspended in outer space as an abstract phenomenon . . . acting under some Satanic inspiration unrelated to any specific motivation.' What is missing, says this former US National Security Advisor, is 'the simple fact that lurking behind every terrorist act is a specific political antecedent.'[11]

Translated from diplomatic formality into the language of the human heart, 'political antecedent' usually means 'human suffering'. Something traumatic happened to the 'terrorists' or their loved ones before they committed their acts of violence. Wherever terrorism chronically occurs – in Northern Ireland, in the Basque region of Spain, in the Israeli–Palestinian conflict, in Kashmir, in Chiapas (Mexico) or Mindanao (the Philippines) – it is preceded by traumatic triggering events.

Let us think, for a moment, about our 'enemies' – whoever we consider them to be. Can we witness their world? Can we learn something about their history of suffering? Can we connect to their loss and grief? And, finally, can we discover ways, no matter how small, to partner with them in our common interest?

As a concrete example, take the relationship between the Western and Eastern superpowers, the United States and the People's Republic of China. Countless recent books by Western 'China experts' – with alarming titles such as *The Coming China Wars*, *Showdown: Why China Wants War with the United States* and *America's Coming War With China* – portray this ancient nation as an emerging 'enemy'. Because of China's growing economic power and increased military spending, some global security experts in the US and Europe assume that China is flexing its muscles and preparing to expand its empire. They advise Western powers to 'contain' China and, in some cases, to invest in more military bases and stronger defence systems in Asia.[12]

If we get to know our 'enemy', however, a different perspective on the Chinese emerges. One discovers a nation that is extremely concerned about its *internal* security situation, with very little energy or ambition for external exploits. Objectively, the USA and Europe are not surrounded by Chinese military installations, while China is, in fact, enveloped on all sides by a

Western military presence. From Afghanistan in the West, to the Philippines, Japan, and South Korea, to a host of aircraft carriers positioned strategically in nearby waters, the Chinese are encircled by troops and weapons belonging to a foreign power. (The USA, for example, has over seven hundred military 'sites' outside its own borders. Since there are only a hundred and ninety-two nations in the world, that is an average of more than three military installations per country!) If we 'walk in their shoes', even for a few steps, we will find many ways to engage our so-called enemy in a promising, fruitful, honest relationship.

9. Transform stereotypes into relationships.

On a leadership course that I co-founded with Outward Bound International, we took twenty emerging leaders on an expedition to the peak of Mount Kilimanjaro. After ten days' trekking, sleeping in tents together and struggling side by side to stay alert despite altitude sickness at 19,000 feet, we knew each other quite well. What became clear to everyone was that the four Muslims – from Oman, Afghanistan, the Philippines, and India – were as different from each other as anyone else in our group. 'They' did not fit a stereotype; and neither did 'we'.

Sometimes reading an insightful novel about them, or watching a powerful film that evokes their history, can open our eyes. But almost always, knowing one's enemy more than superficially requires direct contact. One of the most active leaders of the Czech citizens' movement that fought valiantly against communist domination was Vaclav Havel, a playwright who wrote for the stage what the Soviet authorities prevented being said in the public square. (He later became President of

Czechoslovakia and then the Czech Republic.) Perhaps he best summarized this GI-building practice when he advised each global citizen to ground his views 'not only in sociological statistics, but in real people' and to follow 'not only an adopted ideology, but also his own soul'.[13]

'Try to avoid abstractions,' advises Shlomo Hasson, a leading bridge-builder between Israelis and Palestinians. 'I try, and would advise my fellow citizens to try, to find a friend, a family, on the other side. To learn about their lives, their stories. Don't learn just through statistics or through political analysis. Don't try to "fix" the other side through superficial or instrumental economic or political interventions. Listen to them and their life stories. This will make you care about them and want justice for them, just as you want it for your own flesh and blood.'[14]

10. Ask questions that stretch your mind.

In this book, I have raised questions that have expanded my own understanding of the world. In my experience, asking – or *being* asked – a powerful question can stretch one's mind and increases one's GI more effectively than almost anything.

Several years ago, for example, I was reading a report about trade practices when I encountered an interview with Nawaz Hazari, an uneducated, poor sewing-machine operator in the Ganakbari export-processing zone. This zone, located near Dhaka, Bangladesh, is devoted to producing products for foreign sale. 'Work in the factory is hard,' Nawaz told an English-speaking visitor through translators. 'We are not well treated. *Do people in your country think about our condition when they buy the shirts we make?*'[15]

To this day, I have never forgotten her question because it disturbed me so deeply. I had been wearing shirts made in Asia for many years and had never stopped to ask myself that question. Of course I had thought abstractly about unfair labour practices and the rights of workers. But I had not actually thought specifically about the real human beings who make my clothes. Awakened by her question, I began looking at the labels, learning more about working conditions, and taking these issues into account as a consumer.

Here are three more mind-stretching, heart-opening questions that can challenge us to raise our GI:

How would you control the spread of nuclear weapons?

Ever since 1945, when the first atomic bombs were dropped at the end of World War II, the question of how to control nuclear weapons has been at the front of humanity's negotiating table. Russia and the United States have more than 90 per cent of the world's nuclear weapons.[16] Most of the rest of the world wants these two nations to decrease their stockpiles. These two nations (in their own particular national styles) want other non-nuclear nations to sign and ratify an agreement not to develop nuclear weapons first. How would you negotiate a breakthrough on this stalemate? And how you would do it *soon* before the spread of nuclear-generated electricity makes almost every nation a potential producer of these diabolic weapons – and makes it easier for non-state terrorist groups to access them?

How would you reduce poverty while protecting the environment?

If you have access to the Web, please put the words 'bottom of the pyramid' in your browser and scroll through some of the more than one hundred thousand entries. Doing so will give you direct access to many of the thinkers who are currently grappling with the plight of the billions of people living on two dollars a day.

Challenge yourself to think about how these neighbours of ours in the global village can raise their standard of living, and how they can do so in ways that will not destroy the natural environment on which they depend.

How can impoverished families improve their standard of living in sustainable ways? And what is the ethical responsibility of the more affluent to assist them?

How would you prepare for the intensifying water shortage?

Today one billion people lack safe drinking water. With population increase and climate change, that number will skyrocket.[17] In Asia, for example, more than two billion people depend on their fresh water from the Himalayan watershed. If, as predicted, the glacier ice is reduced by 80 per cent by the year 2030, those two billion people will be in particular peril. Given the near certainty that conflict over water will be a vital issue in the coming decades, what would you do to deal with this looming crisis on the horizon?

If these three questions intrigued you, please select other questions that open your mind. Seek questions that are challenging enough to inspire you to learn, but not so challenging that they make your mind turn off. Remember: the goal is to stretch your mind – not overwhelm it.

11. When the Earth speaks, listen.

When Arctic and Antarctic ice that has been frozen for centuries melts; when entire pods of dolphins are washed up on the beach, dying in huge numbers; when the rate of respiratory diseases increases dramatically in cities during high pollution alerts; when the number of killer hurricanes, heat waves, and other weather phenomena spike – the Earth is telling us something. But are we listening?

In the current negotiations about climate change, human beings in unprecedented numbers are discussing the fate of the Earth. Rich nations are negotiating with poor nations, powerful multinational corporations are negotiating with governments, environmentalists are negotiating with business leaders. More human beings are engaged in a global-policy conversation than ever before. But are we listening to the Earth itself?

As a tropical ecologist and conservation biologist from Tanzania, raised at the foot of Mount Kilimanjaro, Nobby Cordeiro has noticed a strange paradox in his field. 'The scientists who write about tropical forests, and the journals in which they publish, are overwhelmingly based in the North,' he said to a gathering of his peers at the University of Marburg in Germany, with the data carefully presented on the PowerPoint behind the podium. 'With the exception of Brazil and Mexico, the information about the tropics is being gathered and disseminated by scientists in Europe and North America. How can we listen to the Earth if we are handing a fraction of humanity a megaphone and turning the volume down on the rest!'[18]

Listening to the Earth, then, means listening to all its residents – particularly those who often lack a voice. This includes not only the disenfranchised parts of our own species, but the flora and fauna that are not represented in the halls of power. As global citizens, our 'motherland' or 'fatherland' is not just our country. It is the whole, living planet. So listening to her is one of the most important commitments a global citizen can make. Ultimately, she may teach us things that no one else can.

12. Focus patiently on what works.

This way of raising our GI may appear at first glance to be the least exciting, but it is also absolutely vital. Focusing on what works, with genuine patience, can be an antidote to one of the most common toxins of global intelligence: despair.

As we learn more about the world, we become aware of a lot of sad and frightening news.

'So what's the state of the world today?' *Ode Magazine* asked Lester Brown, founder of the Earth Policy Institute.

'We're seeing eroding soils,' he replied, 'falling water tables, collapsing fisheries, shrinking forests, expanding deserts and deteriorating grasslands.' And then he continued with a litany of other negative trends including 'rising temperatures, which affect crop yields and lead to rising sea levels'.[19]

Brown's facts are probably correct. But when they are assembled and presented in this way, do they depress or inspire? As global citizens, we must be careful not to trigger in others, if not in ourselves, a desperate voice that says: 'Things are so bad that all my efforts to make the world a better place will achieve nothing in the long run – so I might as well do nothing!'

Even among 'save the world' activists, it can become very chic to despair. Whoever has the direst diagnosis is considered to be the best informed. We are so proud of being 'globally literate' about what is unfair and wrong, problematic and negative, that we have lost touch with what is beautiful and right, promising and positive. We become addicted to what does not work.

This addiction is fed by the mass media. If a village explodes in violence in Kenya, we see the pictures and read the stories about women and children burnt alive while taking refuge in a church, and we are horrified. When things *don't* work in a spectacular, often violent way, they make the news. Then we pay attention.

But what if a village in Kenya more than doubles its yield of grain per unit of land, increases the amount of land planted, then quadruples its grain production in less than two years? What if the number of malaria cases drops to almost zero? What if children's attendance at school, thanks to a midday feeding programme and other support, increases significantly? And what if similarly remarkable results occur, not just in one village, but in every village that is part of the Millennium Village Project (MVP)?[20]

The fact that MVP has received so little attention and so little money – despite its remarkable success fighting poverty in sub-Saharan Africa – should make us concerned. A church with one hundred people can be burned down in a matter of minutes and images of the heart-rending tragedy can circle the globe in a matter of hours. But turning a village around from despair to hope, and dependence to self-reliance, takes years. What works often requires *patience*.

Paying attention to what works can raise our GI as much as, if not more than, learning about what doesn't.

13. Do it across borders.

Engineers do it. So do architects, news reporters, and teachers. And so do clowns, rock bands, and – as evidenced by the Nobel Peace Prize awarded to Doctors Without Borders – physicians.

As different as these professions are, they can all be practised across borders. In order to emphasize that their profession is made up of global citizens whose responsibility does not stop at the borders of their respective countries, they have created organizations called Engineers Without Borders, Bands Without

Borders, Philanthropists Without Borders, Médecins sans Frontières, and others.

Once a profession goes cross-boundary, it changes. Engineers Without Borders, for example, point out that 90 per cent of their profession is focused on problems that affect only 10 per cent of the world's population. Similarly, Doctors Without Borders address the injustice that the vast majority of medical research is focused on diseases that affect only the most affluent fraction of humanity. Because these organizations work across borders, they do not get trapped in one culture's definition of 'medicine' or 'engineering'. Instead, they work for the whole.

From my own personal experience, I know that, whatever you do, doing it 'across borders' will change both you and your profession. In 1986, I brought filmmakers from the USA and the USSR together in an 'Entertainment Summit' to form an organization that worked to end the cold war on the big screen by fostering collaboration between the Soviet and American film industries. Twenty years later, while working for a global policy think-tank in New York and Brussels called the EastWest Institute, my colleagues and I organized a 'worldwide network of think-tanks' so that these well-connected and well-intentioned enterprises could help each other think – and act – more globally. These and other experiences have taught me that, almost whatever we want to do in our short and precious life, we should learn how to 'do it across borders'.

14. Think both profits *and* values.

We can concentrate on making money or honouring global values. But if we want to raise our GI, it makes more sense to think about both.

The goal of making profits alone will not boost executive GI. Corporate global intelligence will rise much faster if our businesses operate with a triple bottom line: not just profits, but also people and planet. By thinking not just economically, but also socially and environmentally, global citizens in business will raise their GI – and probably their revenues as well. In the words of Google's former executive director Larry Brilliant: don't think in terms of 'traditional profit', but rather of 'social profit'.[21]

During the early years of the AIDS crisis, for example, pharmaceutical companies were attacked by activists for their cold-hearted refusal to lower prices from levels that condemned many African patients to unnecessary suffering and death. Fortunately, thanks to intervention by the Clinton Foundation and other third parties, CEOs of the pharmaceutical companies realized that they could lower prices to a 'no-profit' level in poor countries while maintaining their patent-protected prices in high-income markets. After Merck pharmaceuticals took this step, employees in the company responded with renewed enthusiasm and, according to their CEO at the time, Ray Gilmartin, the company experienced its biggest boost in morale that he had ever seen.[22]

This response should not surprise us. As powerful as the incentive of money can be, it is nowhere near as powerful as money multiplied by meaning. Yet many multinational corporations are still not clear about the global values for which they stand. They project an image of an institution that cares only about its profits, or its return on investment, or increasing its market share. Today they are learning that a company that provides a return on financial investment without global values, if competing against another equally successful company with such values, will ultimately lose global market share.

If given a chance to work for – or buy from – a company that offers both money *and* meaning, global citizens will choose that brand every time.

15. Travel far from – and close to – home.

Global citizens do not measure travel in terms of miles or kilometres alone. 'Travelling' does not necessarily mean dashing through a global landscape. It also means digging into one's local terrain. If we look closely, the whole world is often present near to wherever we call home. In addition to travelling 'abroad', we can also travel 'at home'.

Many local communities are like seeds that contain within them the tree of humanity. Knowing the local is one of the best ways to know the global. If you live in a city of significant size, the whole world is outside your doorstep. Dig beneath the surface of Curitiba (Brazil) or Chicago (USA), Bogotá (Colombia) or Mumbai (India), and you will discover an 'integral city' that contains the whole world in microcosm.[23] You don't need an aeroplane ticket to visit the world, just a city bus pass!

In fact, for most citizens in developed countries, the wider world is as close as your local supermarket and the shelves in your kitchen. Trace even the most ordinary products, such as your morning cup of coffee or the bananas you slice onto your cereal, back to their source and you encounter a global travelogue filled with rich complexity. If we want coffee and banana farmers around the world to have a living wage, then we can be part of the solution by ensuring that the products we purchase are based on the principles of fair trade: fair prices for small farmers, good wages and working conditions for plantation workers, the rights of workers to organize, and sustainable agricultural practices.[24] And once you learn the lessons of those supply chains, you can study the petrol in your car, the wood in your home, or the microchips in the computer at your local cybercafe. If you do, you may suddenly discover the whole world.

The truth is: our local culture is often more global than it first appears. Look at those who govern your community or nation, for example. Whether you live in the People's Republic of China or the United Kingdom, in Germany, France, or the United States, look at the people in your legislature or parliament. You will notice that they tend to be much more uniform than the people whom they represent.

So one way that global citizens can travel without leaving home is to make sure that your local institutions begin to honour the 'glocal' realities. Help to bring your local diversity into the halls of power. If you bear witness to your own community, you will almost certainly find the world *within* it.

16. Seek common ground.

What do the American and Chinese cultures have in common?

This question is vitally important to the course of the twenty-first century for a very simple reason. If these two cultures find nothing in common, they will find no common ground and we are all in trouble. But if they share at least something, then they can build on that common foundation.

Fortunately, underneath some profound differences, these two great cultures do have cultural common ground. According to the GLOBE study, the Chinese and American views of leadership are extremely different and extremely similar. In terms of attitude toward authority, no two cultures could be more different. If we want to create tension between these two great nations, there are many wedges we can drive between them in this area. However, these same two cultures have some attitudes that are absolutely shared. Both of them, according to the lead researcher, Mansour Javidan, have an extremely high 'perform-ance orientation'. Both care deeply about results, and both today's Chinese and Americans want to be rewarded based on actual accomplishments, not status or rank.[25]

As this data demonstrates, we have a choice. Whatever the differences between human beings may be, we can focus on what divides us, or on what connects us. Finding common ground creates possibilities. Seeking out what is universal therefore raises our global intelligence because it compels us to look beneath the obvious, and sometimes aggravating, differences to discover the hidden (and often rewarding) commonalities.

As global citizens, we don't need to minimize differences, but we do need to learn about what all people share. We need to search for common ground – and that, in turn, requires another practice.

17. Speak more than one language.

As children, we grow up speaking a language that enables us to communicate to some of our fellow human beings, but not to others. The language (or in some communities, the languages) that we learn when we are young occupies a unique position in our brain physiology: it becomes the lens through which we view the world. It shapes us in ways that neurolinguists are only now discovering.

At the Thunderbird School of Global Management, for example, the faculty tries 'to teach students how to read *how the world works'*. With thirty-eight thousand alumni in a hundred and forty-one countries, Thunderbird – like other leading international business schools such as INSEAD in Paris and Singapore – promotes global literacy as a key part of its curriculum.

Thunderbird is a leader in cross-boundary learning because, while located in the USA, it still manages to create a global learning environment. According to Dr Angel Cabrera, its president, top European business schools are 'intrinsically more international than their US counterparts'. As an example, he cites a school in Holland which, 'by necessity, will have a student body comprising five or six different countries and those students are going to come in with three or four languages'. To create a similar kind of cross-boundary environment, Thunderbird requires foreign-language training.

'You can train people in cross-cultural communication,' says Cabrera, 'but it is harder to get them to understand what cross-cultural relations are if those people have never struggled with learning a foreign language.'[26]

In addition to learning more than one *culture*-based language, we also need to learn to communicate with other *belief*-based languages. For example, some people speak the theological language of the Bible or the Koran. Others speak the corporate language of bottom lines, ROIs, and market shares. Still others speak the language of the law and rights.

So do not presume that everybody – even everybody in your own linguistic group – speaks your 'language'. One of the best investments you can make is to learn to speak the language of the people you want to reach.

If requiring a foreign language for a degree in 'global management' sounds obvious to you, keep in mind that, until recently, very few CEOs in the West were multilingual. Even most

Presidents of the United States have never been able to speak a language other than English fluently. So the recognition that a second, or even a third, language makes a business executive more effective represents a critical, if elementary, step in raising our GI.

18. Learn to see through walls.

Two feuding brothers may build a wall through an orchard, separating it into two. But the fruit is still the same; the roots are still in the same earth; the same bees will pollinate the blossoms; the same sun will shine on their leaves. No matter how high they make the wall, and even if they fortify it with barbed wire or defend it with armed guards or dig deep trenches around it, their wall does not demarcate the end of the orchard. On the other side of the wall, it continues.

Wherever you or I sit right now, something stops our vision from extending throughout the world. It may be the physical walls of an apartment building or school or institution. Or it may be the political walls of cities or states and countries or regions, or the economic walls of wealth and poverty, privilege and oppression. If not these barriers, then it may be the mental walls of attitudes and ideologies, dogmas or belief systems. Wherever we live, there are walls which block our vision – if not of oppression, then of privilege; if not of ignorance, then of sensationalized and incomplete information.

But from an aeroplane or a spaceship, or via images transmitted from a cell phone camera, we can see on the other side of the walls. We know from our personal experience that a wall cannot block our vision. Indeed, we have a skill that sounds like a superhero's: we can see through walls.

19. Explore the mysteries of the sacred.

Discovering what our fellow human beings hold sacred – and why – is one of the most important GI-building journeys we can undertake. Since human intelligence alone will never unravel all the riddles of creation, the sacred practices of the cultures of mankind are vital sources of wisdom that our species needs in order to survive and flourish.

I have attended Catholic Mass in Paris, Shabbat services in Israel, and sacred dances in Indonesia. Around the world I have bowed and prayed in mosques, held the Torah in synagogues, and recited psalms from the Bible in churches. I have practised Buddhist meditation and recited ancient Hindu mantras. And after a lifetime of exploring the sacred traditions of the world, I bow in reverence, more deeply than ever, before the great mystery.

My life has taught me that the sacred knows no borders. It is everywhere. I can't always recognize it, or understand it. But it is there in every culture in the world.

When thirty-two bishops met to replace Desmond Tutu as the Anglican Archbishop of Southern Africa, they agreed to set ground rules for the deliberations. 'We must listen to one another,' said one bishop.

'No, brother, that's not quite it,' said a second bishop. 'We must listen with empathy.'

'That's still not enough,' said a third. 'We must listen to the *sacred* in one another.'

If we focus on the 'sacred in one another', we discover that we are all connected not only by our genes, but by our souls. When we filter out the narrow, manmade, 'tribal' elements of the various faiths, we are left standing in awe at the shared spiritual heritage of humankind. All the faiths have a golden rule, and following this golden thread will more deeply connect our global intelligence to our souls.[27]

20. Global citizens, unite!

To raise our GI effectively, we need to work with others in geo-partnerships. The best way to learn is to find a partner and get to work. Learning how to collaborate with other human beings around the world is the ultimate test of our global intelligence.

Based on my experience, I know that there are tens of millions of people, from every nation and with every colour of skin and in every profession, who are global citizens. I have met some of them all over the world: in cafes in Amman; in an international school in Hong Kong; in a Kenyan village; at a corporate retreat in Texas; on the trails of Mount Kilimanjaro; and in the halls of parliaments and legislatures throughout the world. Everywhere, I experience this yearning to connect beyond the borders that divide us.

Wherever we live, let us find these global neighbours. Let us explore what we can do beyond borders that we cannot possibly do within them. Working separately, barricaded behind walls, our fate is sealed. But working together, the possibility of a truly just and sustainable global civilization has never been more alive than today. By reaching out to each other, we can transform that possibility into a living reality.

Global Citizens' Resources:

An Action Guide

This Action Guide, co-written with Katia Nysti, includes at least two or more resources for each of the GI-raising strategies mentioned in the conclusion. Given its English language and Western orientation, it is not intended to be a comprehensive list, but rather a starting point for taking action. Please enrich this list by consulting Websites in your language and through your own cultural resources. If you are looking for additional resources, please visit www.mediatorsfoundation.org. There you will find a richer, more up-to-date listing.

In addition, my colleagues and I offer a workshop, 'The Global Citizen Experience', based directly on this book, which includes a specific set of educational and training opportunities that are designed for three primary audiences: educators, corporate executives, and inter-governmental agencies.

For more information about this workshop, go to www.mediatorsfoundation.org.

1. Be the change that you want to see.

Avaaz

With the tagline 'the world in action', this high-powered progressive network organizes action on key global issues. It actively and proudly 'takes sides' on what its members consider to be the key moral issues of our time.
http://www.avaaz.org/

Edmund J. Bourne, *Global Shift: How a New Worldview Is Transforming Humanity* (Oakland, CA: Noetics Books / New Harbinger Publications, 2008).
This book provides an opportunity to reflect deeply on how one's inner life is responding to the global crises we face. Read it to deepen your awareness of this moment in history and how it affects us all.

Ed and Deb Shapiro, *Be The Change: How Meditation Can Transform You and the World* (New York: Sterling Ethos, 2009); Stephen M. Shick, ***Be the Change: Poems, Prayers, and Meditations for Peacemakers and Justice Seekers*** (Boston, MA: Skinner House Books, 2009)
Because Gandhi's advice is so timely, there are many books that bear this title. These two are particularly useful for awakening us to the connection between our 'inner' state of being and the 'outer' events of the world. These books can make us more aware of how changing ourselves and changing the world are deeply and mysteriously intertwined.

2. Use both sides of your brain.

The HeartMath Institute

The Institute of HeartMath is a non-profit research and
education organization dedicated to heart-based living. Heart-
based living focuses on people relying on the intelligence of
their hearts in connection with their minds to conduct their
lives at home, school, work, and play. You'll find educational
materials and online applications on their Website to help you
experience the physical, mental, and emotional benefits of
heart-based living.
http://www.heartmath.org/

Daniel H. Pink, *A Whole New Mind: Why Right-Brainers Will Rule the Future* (London: Cyan, 2006)

Daniel Pink shares with us six right-brain aptitudes on which
professional success and personal fulfilment now depend. Up
until now much success was dependent on left-brain skills:
today we need both. The book includes a series of hands-on
exercises from experts around the world to help us sharpen
these aptitudes. Applying these practices will change how you
experience the world.

3. Remember that 'one' comes before 'two'.

The Genographic Project

The Genographic Project is using cutting-edge technologies to
analyse historical patterns in DNA from participants around the
world to better understand our human genetic roots. This
project is led by National Geographic Explorer-in-Residence
Dr Spencer Wells and includes a team of renowned

international scientists and researchers.
https://genographic.nationalgeographic.com/genographic/
index.html

Global Oneness Project

Since 2006, the Global Oneness Project has gathered stories
from around the world of people who base their lives and work
on understanding our interconnectedness. They have a full
library of films and educational material available for free from
their Website.
http://www.globalonenessproject.org/

4. Make sure your house has a door.

Education for Global Citizenship

A programme of Oxfam Education, this initiative offers a huge
range of ideas, resources, and support for developing the global
dimension in the classroom and the whole school. All of the
resources here support Education for Global Citizenship –
education that helps pupils understand their world and make a
positive difference in it.
http://www.oxfam.org.uk/education/

**Sara Bullard, *Teaching Tolerance: Raising Open-Minded,
Empathetic Children*** (New York; London: Doubleday, 1996)
Bullard suggests that tolerance begins at home. Raising our
children to draw quick conclusions, ranking people and things
and preferring the familiar, can lead to intolerance. Bullard
looks at how we raise our children and provides us with some
insight on how to support our children to be open minded and
caring towards all of life.

5. Think like a minority.

Global Voices

Global Voices is a community of bloggers who bring you translations and reports from across the globe, with an emphasis on voices that are not ordinarily heard in international mainstream media.
http://globalvoicesonline.org/

Anouar Majid, *We Are All Moors: Ending Centuries of Crusades against Muslims and Other Minorities*
(Minneapolis: University of Minnesota Press, 2009)
This powerful book explores how Europe's historical conflict between the Christians and the Moors has served as a foundation for how we define and relate to minorities across the world. 'Only by recognizing the connections between current fears about immigration and Islam and medieval Christianity's crusade against the Moor', he argues, 'can we begin to redress centuries of oppression, learn from the tragedies of the past, and find common ground in a globalized world.'

6. Increase your knowledge – including how to not-know.

The Globalist

This daily online magazine, available for free to registered users, offers 'a feature on a key global issue written by either our in-house team or a diverse group of contributors. Reaching an audience in more than a hundred and twenty countries around the world, *The Globalist* advances global dialogue and

communicates innovative global thinking.'
www.theglobalist.com

Shunry Suzuki, *Zen Mind, Beginner's Mind* (Boston, MA:
Shambhala, 2006)
Zen Master Suzuki's book is filled with excerpts from his
lectures looking at Beginner's Mind, the nuts and bolts of
meditation as well as selflessness, emptiness, and mindfulness.

7. Test your worldview against the actual facts.

Global Issues

This site is focused on 'Social, Political, Economic and
Environmental Issues That Affect Us All'. In contrast to the UN-
based website (www.un.org/en/globalissues/), which has
considerable organizational support, this website is a heroic
effort by Anup Shah, a single individual, to create greater
awareness about global issues.
http://www.globalissues.org/

**Brooks Jackson and Kathleen Hall Jamieson, *unSpun:
Finding Facts in a World of Disinformation*** (New York:
Random House Trade Paperbacks, 2007)
unSpun is a media literacy crash course. With the Internet and
self-publishing creating more and more information for us to
sift through it isn't often easily apparent what is 'true'. The
book provides us with some awareness of how to identify
when messages have been 'spun' and how to find the facts.

8. Know your enemy – inside and out.

Search for Common Ground

Search for Common Ground works to transform the way the world deals with conflict – 'away from adversarial approaches and towards collaborative problem solving'. It focuses on developing our capacity to understand 'our differences and act on our commonalities'.
http://www.sfcg.org/

Sam Keen, *Faces of the Enemy: Reflections of the Hostile Imagination* (2nd ed., San Francisco, CA: HarperSanFrancisco, 1991)

Sam Keen's book takes a close look at how ordinary and seemingly decent people can be stirred to view their neighbours as enemies. Keen looks at the psychological mechanism of enmity itself and ways to transform these perceptions.

9. Transform stereotypes into relationships.

Rotary International

Rotary is a worldwide service organization of more than 1.2 million business, professional, and community leaders in 33,000 clubs in more than 200 countries. Clubs are non-political, non-religious, and open to all cultures, races, and creeds. Rotary's main objective of service in the community, in the workplace, and throughout the world has provided a bridge to building relationships across both cultures and geographic borders.
www.rotaryinternational.org

World Learning

World Learning is a seventy-five-year-old global non-profit organization operating international education and development programs in more than seventy countries worldwide. It connects young ambassadors annually across cultural differences and social barriers fostering global citizenship.

www.worldlearning.org

10. Ask questions that stretch your mind.

NAFSA: Association of International Educators
European Association for International Education
Asia Society

These are three of the many organizations that are working hard to transform the experience of learning to include global perspectives, not just national agendas. Please explore in your own country what institutions are working to enable learning to extend 'beyond borders'.

www.nafsa.org / www.eaie.org / www.asiasociety.org

World Café

World Café is an innovative and simple methodology for hosting conversations about questions that matter in large group settings. The Website provides educational material, stories and connections to World Café guides around the world.

http://www.theworldcafe.com/

Nayan Chanda, *Bound Together: How Traders, Preachers, Adventurers, and Warriors Shaped Globalization* (New Haven: Yale University Press, 2007)
Read this book and it will trigger many questions about how the world became so interconnected, who is being hurt and helped by that connection, and why we must accelerate our global learning in order to deal with the issues that globalization raises.

11. When the Earth speaks, listen.

The Earth Charter Initiative

The Earth Charter Initiative is a diverse, global network of people, organizations, and institutions that participate in 'promoting and implementing the values and principles of the Earth Charter'. The Earth Charter focuses 'on sustainable ways of living and a shared ethical framework that includes respect and care for the community of life, ecological integrity, universal human rights, respect for diversity, economic justice, democracy, and a culture of peace'.
http://www.earthcharterinaction.org/content/

The Pachamama Alliance

This North–South geo-partnership is based on the recognition that those in the developed world share a deep connection with the people who call the rainforest home. The Alliance recognizes that indigenous people are the rainforests' natural custodians, and therefore key strategies of our alliance focus on strengthening their culture and empowering their ability to stand for and represent their own interests.
www.pachamama.org

Martin Gray, *Sacred Earth: Places of Peace and Power*
(New York: Sterling; Lewes, 2007)
A beautiful book filled with photographs and fascinating text
from acclaimed photographer and anthropologist Martin Gray's
twenty-year journey to a thousand sacred sites in eighty
countries around the world. *Sacred Earth* reveals how cultures
everywhere have worshipped and respected our Earth.

12. Focus patiently on what works.

Appreciative Inquiry Commons

Appreciative Inquiry is a systemic method to 'apprehend,
anticipate and heighten' what is working best in people, their
organizations, and the relevant world around them.
Appreciative Inquiry Commons is a warehouse of information
and resources for anyone wanting to practise this method.
http://appreciativeinquiry.case.edu/

Ode

Both the magazine and online community are about 'the people
and ideas that are changing our world for the better'. They
focus on positive stories about people around the world who
are architects of creative change.
www.odemagazine.com

13. Do it across borders.

e-Parliament

The e-Parliament exists to share 'good policy ideas among the
democratic parliamentarians of the world, and to help build
broad coalitions to implement those ideas'. It has gathered a

database of eighteen thousand members of parliament from
ninety-seven countries.
www.e-parl.net

Global Action Networks

Like Doctors Without Borders and e-Parliament, Global Action
Networks (GANs) are a leading innovation for scaling impact to
address issues of common good globally. GANs are a specific
type of innovation that brings together five strategic qualities:
1. is global; 2. focuses on issues of common public interest
(not profit-seeking); 3. develops interdisciplinary action-
learning with real-time experiments to address novel and
enduring challenges; 4. creates a diverse network of
organizations of stakeholders in their issue; 5. generates
systemic change by creating cross-sectoral (business-
government-civil society) actions.
http://www.scalingimpact.net/gan

Paula Rothenberg, *Beyond Borders: Thinking Critically About Global Issues*

Beyond Borders (http://bcsworthpublishers.com/beyondborders)
provides a series of articles drawn from a variety of disciplines,
written by scholars, activists, and policymakers from around
the world 'exploring the dynamic complexities of life in our
global villages'.

14. Think both profits *and* values.

Center for Global Citizenship

The Ford Motor Company Center for Global Citizenship at the
Kellogg School of Management at Northwestern University

'draws on a diverse array of Kellogg School and Northwestern faculty and researchers to investigate the role of business and its interaction with the social and political environment'. Based on its philosophy that corporations have become 'the main agents of global social and political change', the Center helps corporate leaders deal with global issues with tools including values-based management and triple bottom line.
http://www.kellogg.northwestern.edu/research/fordcenter/

ICLEI – Local Governments for Sustainability

ICLEI Local Governments for Sustainability is an international association of 1,100 local governments from sixty-seven countries who are committed to sustainable development. ICLEI provides educational support to build the capacity of local governments to implement sustainable development at the local level.
http://www.iclei.org

Peter M. Senge et al., *The Necessary Revolution: How individuals and organizations are working together to create a sustainable world* (New York: Doubleday, 2008)

Of the many books about the 'greening of capitalism', this one can serve as a starting point on the journey toward sustainable development. Along with *Natural Capitalism* and *Small Is Beautiful*, it sets the stage for understanding how humanity might, just might, be able to satisfy its material wants while caring for our bio-home.

15. Travel far from – and close to – home.

Global Diversity Foundation

The Global Diversity Foundation 'promotes the richness of local cultures and their environments around the world' through research, training and social action. Focused on long-term community-based projects, the foundation supports the important role diversity has in globalization.
http://www.globaldiversity.org.uk

Mary Pipher, *The Middle of Everywhere: Helping Refugees Enter the American Community* (Boston, MA: Harvest Books, 2003)

Pipher tells the stories of a group of refugees, from a variety of countries, who emigrate to Lincoln, Nebraska. She also describes her own journey connecting, developing friendships and supporting the 'world culture that flourishes in her hometown'.

16. Seek common ground.

A Common Word Between Us and You

In 2007, one hundred and thirty-eight Muslim scholars, clerics, and intellectuals came together to develop a declaration of the common ground between Christianity and Islam. Their declaration was entitled *A Common Word Between Us and You*. Their website includes this document, listing of A Common Word events, endorsements and responses from others, and support for interfaith dialogues all over the world.
http://www.acommonword.com/

Crisis Prevention and Recovery

No single organization in the world does more to prevent violence and promote healing from war than this bureau within the United Nations Development Program. BCPR works around the world to restore the quality of life for those who have been devastated by natural disaster or violent conflict. Operating through more than 100 country offices, the Bureau provides a bridge between the humanitarian agencies that handle immediate needs and the long-term process of peacemaking and rebuilding war-torn societies.
http://www.undp.org/cpr/

Howard Thurman, *The Search for Common Ground*
(Richmond, IN: Friends United Press, 1986)
Howard Thurman encourages us to focus on community, looking beyond our personal identity 'to that which we have in common with all life'. Thurman spent his life building community across racial, cultural, and religious divides.

17. Speak more than one language.

Rosetta Stone

Expand your linguistic intelligence by learning a new language. Rosetta Stone is a leading language-learning software used by learners across the globe. Rosetta Stone focuses on simulating the manner in which people learn their native tongues without translations. http://www.rosettastone.com

John McWhorter, *The Power of Babel: A Natural History of Language* (London: Arrow, 2003)

McWhorter describes the evolution of linguistics that has brought us more than six thousand world 'languages' and that has helped shape us, our cultures, and our nations. A wonderful framework for understanding the constantly changing linguistic evolution we take part in as a global community.

18. Learn to see through walls

Global Citizens Network

GCN works to promote peace, justice, and tolerance through cross-cultural understanding and global cooperation. It is committed to enhancing quality of life around the world while preserving indigenous cultures, traditions and ecologies.
http://www.globalcitizens.org/

Global Studies Association

Since there are more than half a million resources on the Web for 'global studies', a useful starting point is the GSA. It is a multi-disciplinary scholarly association set up to address the vast social, political, and economic transformations of global scope which are impacting upon the world today. The GSA provides a forum for scholars to collaborate and explore shared responses to such phenomena, particularly in the context of globalization.
http://www.globalstudiesassociation.org/

19. Explore the mysteries of the sacred.

Abraham Path

The Abraham Path is a cultural itinerary that inspires and engages travellers to journey on the national and local trails of each nation of the Middle East, following in the footsteps of Abraham himself. Walking this path, together with others of different faiths, is an opportunity to experience and promote the healing between the Abrahamic faiths.
www.abrahampath.org

United Religions Initiative

United Religions Initiative (URI) is a global community of local 'Cooperation Circles' spanning over sixty-five countries and representing more than a hundred religions, spiritual expressions, and indigenous traditions. It is committed to 'promoting enduring, daily interfaith cooperation and to ending religiously motivated violence'.
http://www.uri.org/

Philip Novak, *The World's Wisdom: Sacred Texts of the World's Religions* (San Francisco, CA: HarperSanFrancisco, 1994)

A collection of sacred texts of the religions of the world, written as a companion for Huston Smith's *The Religions of Man*. Chapters include Hinduism, Buddhism, Confucianism, Taoism, Judaism, Christianity, Islam, and Primal religions (e.g. Native American, African, etc.).

20. Global citizens, unite!

Clinton Global Initiative

Building on President Clinton's lifetime in public service, the Clinton Global Initiative (CGI) reflects his belief that governments need collaboration from the private sector, non-governmental organizations, and other global leaders to effectively confront the world's most pressing problems.
www.clintonglobalinitiative.org/

Global Citizen Center

The centre serves activists who share an intention to 'realign the world's social and political agenda so that problems are solved by putting the common interest of the whole world's people ahead of the special interest of nations, corporations, religions or individuals'. It also publishes *Global Journal* and hosts the blog Global Talk.
http://globalcitizencenter.net/

Wiser Earth

WiserEarth is a free online community space connecting the people, non-profits, and businesses working toward a just and sustainable world. This invaluable website includes 320 specific resources under 'global citizenship' and 2,124 for 'global citizen'. Although it is heavily North American in focus, it is nevertheless an outstanding starting point for becoming familiar with many organizations that are putting global citizenship into action.
http://www.wiserearth.org/

Notes

Introduction

[1] Bono, 'Rebranding Africa', *New York Times*, 10 July 2009.
[2] Samuel Palmisano, 'The Globally Integrated Enterprise', *Foreign Affairs*, May–June 2006, p. 131.
[3] Mansour Javidan's comments are partly from the breakfast conversation, and from a subsequent interview on 11 February 2008.
[4] This 2008 poll was conducted by World Public Opinion. For more information about this attitude survey, go to WorldPublicOpinion.org or contact the Program on International Policy Attitudes at the University of Maryland.
[5] Vinay Bhargava, ed., *Global Issues for Global Citizens* (World Bank: Washington, DC, 2006).

1. Witnessing

[1] The full story is available at http://www.newsweek.com/id/69585/output/print.
[2] Kevin W. Kelley, *The Home Planet* (Reading, MA: Addison Wesley, 1988) is the source of all these quotes except one. The Israeli astronaut's comments were cited in B. K. S. Iyengar, *Light on Life: The Journey to Wholeness, Inner Peace and Ultimate Freedom* (London: Rodale Press, 2005), p. 16.
[3] I describe this process more fully in my book *Leading Through Conflict* (Boston, MA: Harvard Business School Press, 2006), Chapter 3, 'Presence'. It is also well described in Peter Senge et al., *Presence*, and in Otto Scharmer's *Theory U: Leading From the Future as It Emerges: The Social Technology of Presencing* (Cambridge, MA: SoL, The Society for Organizational Learning, 2007).

[4] I am grateful to Thomas Putnam, Director of the John F. Kennedy Presidential Library and Museum, for providing me with a transcript of President Kennedy's remarks and of Gordon Brown's speech.

[5] Peter Eisler, 'Commercial satellites alter global security', *USA Today*, 7 November 2008, p. 13A.

[6] Marianne Berecz, 'Open, Safe and Secure: Managing borders in the OSCE area', *OSCE Magazine*, July 2006.

[7] John L. Esposito and Dalia Mogahed, *Who Speaks For Islam? What A Billion Muslims Really Think* (New York: Gallup Press, 2007), pp. 69–70.

[8] I want to acknowledge the work of Ken Wilber and Don Beck as precursors of this formulation of Citizen 1.0–5.0. Both Wilber's writing on egocentric, sociocentric, and worldcentric perspectives and Beck's analysis of 'first-tier' and 'second-tier' worldviews were building blocks for this section of this chapter. I want to express my sincere gratitude to both of these pioneering thinkers.

[9] For a US case study, see my *A House Divided: Six Belief Systems Struggling for America's Soul* (New York: Tarcher/Putnam, 1996).

[10] Kenneth Ross quoted in Robin Wright, 'The New Tribalism', *Los Angeles Times*, 8 June 1992, cited in Miroslav Volf, *Exclusion & Embrace* (Nashville: Abingdon Press, 1996), p. 15.

[11] Albert Einstein, *The World As I See It* (trans. Alan Harris, London: J. Lane, 1935).

[12] Thabo Mbeki, 'I am an African', 1996. A speech made on behalf of the ANC on the occasion of the adoption by the Constitutional Assembly of the Republic of South Africa Constitution Bill 1996, 8 May 1996. I am grateful to Ms Sibongile Muthwa of Durban for providing me with this transcript.

[13] Jodi Kantor, 'Nation's Many Faces in Extended First Family', *New York Times*, 21 January 2009, p. 1.

14 Merry M. Merryfield, 'The Difference a Global Educator Can Make', *Educational Leadership*, October 2002.

15 Cited in Sir John Marks Templeton, *Worldwide Laws Of Life* (Philadelphia and London: Templeton Foundation Press, 1997), p. 487.

16 Joel Gershon, 'L.A. professor triggers Myanmar Web shutdown', Reuters/*Hollywood Reporter*, 4 October 2007.

17 *Yahoo News* (http://news.yahoo.com/;_ylt=AlPVjr_ yo8BiaJJQbgjV2pf9xg8F).

18 Go to www.witness.org to see video footage of incidents of injustice around the world.

19 Paul Hawken, *Blessed Unrest* (New York : Penguin Books), p. 147.

20 These images are available at http://hungary1956.com/audiovideo/NewsMagazine_1957_ HungarianRevolution.avi.

21 D. T. Max, 'The Making of the Speech', *New York Times*, 7 October 2001.

22 Mohamad Bazzi, 'War on the Corner', *New York Times Magazine*, 5 October 2008, p. 86.

23 Richard E. Nesbit, *The Geography of Thought: How Asians and Westerners Think Differently – and Why* (New York: Free Press, 2008).

24 David Brooks, 'A Network of Truces', *New York Times*, 8 April 2008, p. A27; citing as a source Philip Carl Salzman, *Culture and Conflict in the Middle East* (Amherst, NY: Humanity Books, 2008).

25 Scilla Elworthy, *Fallujah* (unpublished paper analysing the US-led invasion of the city).

26 Dexter Filkins, *The Forever War* (New York: Knopf, 2008).

27 This chapter is informed by the concept of 'social memes' as developed by Don Beck in his (and Christopher Cowan's) *Spiral Dynamics: mastering values, leadership and change* (Oxford: Blackwell, 1996) and the concept of 'mental models'

as used by my colleagues Peter Senge et al. in their extremely helpful work *The Fifth Discipline Fieldbook* (New York: Currency, Doubleday, 1994). Senge defines worldviews as 'the semi-permanent tacit "maps" of the world which people hold in their long-term memory, and the short-term perceptions which people build up as a part of their everyday reasoning'.

2. Learning

1. Lawrence Wright, *The Looming Tower: Al-Qaeda and the road to 9/11* (New York: Knopf, 2006), Chapter 1.
2. Thich Nhat Hanh, *Calming the Fearful Mind* (Berkeley, CA: Parallax Press, 2005), pp. 9–10.
3. To find out more about his community in France, contact pvlistening@plumvill.net.
4. Dalai Lama, 'My Vision of a Compassionate Future', *Washington Post*, 21 October 2007.
5. This banker was quoted in Thomas Friedman, 'Give them a voice', *International Herald Tribune*, 31 October 2002.
6. Joshua Cooper Ramo, *The Age of the Unthinkable* (Boston: Little Brown, 2009), p. 8.
7. For further information, contact Andy Nagorski at the EastWest Institute, the organization that hosted these meetings. www.ewi.info.
8. Nicholas Wade, 'Eden? Maybe. But Where's the Apple Tree?', *New York Times*, 1 May 2009, p. A6.
9. Quoted in Nayan Chanda, *Bound Together* (Yale University Press: New Haven), 2000.
10. Ibid., p. 21.
11. Luis Quintana-Murci quoted in Gary Stix, 'Traces of a Distant Past', *Scientific American*, July 2008, p. 63.
12. Frances Drabick, 'About Legacy', *AARP Bulletin*, September 2009, p. 30.
13. 'Army Stage-Managed Fall of Hussein Statue', David Zucchino,

Los Angeles Times, July 03, 2004. Further video evidence is available on www.youtube.com.

[14] Fred Kaplan, 'National styles of pulling down statues', posted Wednesday, 9 April 2003, at 11:14 ET.

[15] Another recent example of this was the competing versions of events in Tibet. When the Chinese cracked down on protesting monks and their supporters in Lhasa, the military manoeuvres ordered from Beijing were largely hidden from view by the Chinese, who controlled media coverage. But a quick scan of YouTube reveals scores of homemade videos taken by tourists who shared their experience globally via the Internet. If one turns to these videos and other articles by pro-Tibetan observers, the official Chinese version is challenged.

[16] Mark Gerzon, *Leading Through Conflict: How Successful Leaders Transform Differences Into Opportunities* (Boston, MA: Harvard Business School Press, 2006).

[17] Mohandas K. Gandhi, *Bread Labour: The Gospel of Work* (Ahmedabad: 1960).

[18] *The Bhagavad Gita According to Gandhi*, edited by John Strohmeier (Berkeley, CA: Berkeley Hills Books, 2000), p. 48.

[19] Elaine Woo, 'Yoga guru Swami Satchadinanda dies', *Los Angeles Times*, reprinted in the *Daily Camera*, 25 August 2002.

[20] Maximilian Johnson, 'Unrivalled access to the next superpower', *Financial Times*, 2 February 2009, p. 12.

[21] The quotations from Bishop, Dekkers and Kathwari are from Louise Story, 'Seeking Leaders, U.S. Companies Think Globally', *New York Times*, 12 December 2007.

[22] From a conversation between a CEO of a major Chinese company with the author at a recent Harvard Business Review Roundtable, May 2008.

[23] Anil Gupta, Vijay Govindarajan and Haiyan Wang, 'The Quest for Global Dominance', *Globalist*, 2 April 2008.

[24] Louise Story, op. cit. note 21.

[25] Ron Moffatt quoted in Darlene Bremer, 'Wanted Global:

International education experiences help prepare global-ready graduates for the twenty-first-century workforce', *International Educator*, May–June 2006, pp. 40–45.

26 'National Policies for International Education', in *The Networker: The International Education Magazine* (Fall 2007), published by the Institute of International Education, New York, p. 22.

27 Samuel Palmisano, 'The Globally Integrated Enterprise', *Foreign Affairs*, May–June 2006, p. 131.

28 Ibid., p. 131.

29 Interview with Yves Doz in *Strategy + Business*, Issue 29, pp. 115ff. For a fuller account of his thinking, see his recent book, co-authored with Jose Santos and Peter Williamson, *From Global To Metanational: How Companies Win in the Knowledge Economy* (Boston, MA: Harvard Business School Press, 2001).

30 Dilip Murkerjea, *Surfing the Intellect: Building Intellectual Capital for a Knowledge Economy* (Singapore: Brainware Press, Mui Kee Press).

31 See http://www.e-learningcentre.co.uk/eclipse/Resources/quotations.htm.

32 Peter Senge, 'The Leader's New Work: Building Learning Organizations', *Sloan Management Review* 7 (Fall 1990). The themes in this article were developed in Senge's numerous books, including *The Fifth Discipline* and *The Fifth Discipline Fieldbook*.

33 Frances Cairncross, *The Death of Distance* (Boston, MA: Harvard Business School Press: 1997).

3. Connecting

1 'Bush voices regret for macho rhetoric', *Guardian*, 11 June 2008.

2 To witness the video *Fitna*, simply enter its title on www.youtube.com.

3   To see one example of a rebuttal, see
    www.youtube.com/watch?v=NV2uITx6QCs.
4   Robert Marquand, 'Dutch Leader's Anti-Islam Film Brings
    Strife', *Christian Science Monitor*, 28 March 2008; Gregory
    Crouch, 'Dutch Film is Released on Internet', *New York Times*,
    28 March 2008; and John F. Burns, 'Britain Refuses Entry to
    Dutch Lawmaker Whose Remarks and Film Have Angered
    Muslims', *New York Times*, 14 June 2009.
5   http://www.whitehouse.gov/the_press_office/Remarks-by-the-
    President-at-Cairo-University-6-04-09/
6   The Clarion Fund lists as its mailing address 38 State Street,
    Portsmouth, NH 03801, and its phone number as
    888.610.2221. For more information, contact it at
    info@clarionfund.org.
7   To view this disrespectful, distorting film, go to
    http://www.obsessionthemovie.com.
8   To watch Senator Obama give this historic speech, go to
    www.youtube.com/watch?v=pWe7wTVbLUU - 144k.
9   Barack Obama, *The Audacity of Hope* (New York: Crown,
    2006), p. 3.
10 Gérard Chaliand and Jean-Pierre Rageau, *The Penguin Atlas of
    Diasporas* (New York: Viking, 1995) lists twelve: Lebanese,
    Jewish, Armenian, Gypsy, Black, Chinese, Indian, Irish,
    Greek, Balkan, Vietnamese and Korean. While this is a
    tremendously useful broadening of the concept of diasporas
    (many Westerners apply the term only to the Jewish case), it
    still underestimates the full extent of human movement.
11 Amin Maalouf, *In the Name of Identity: Violence and the Need to
    Belong* (English translation of *Les Identités meurtrières*, Paris:
    Grasset. 1998).
12 These genocides include:
    • Europe under Nazi Germany and Adolf Hitler, 1933–45
      (6 million deaths)
    • Poland under the Soviet Union, 1940s (2.5 million deaths)

- Cambodia under Pol Pot, 1975–79 (2 million-plus deaths)
- Armenia under Turkey, 1915–23 (1.5 million deaths)
- Tibet under the Chinese Communist Party, 1949–50 (1.2 million deaths)
- Rwanda, 1994 (800,000 deaths)
- the ongoing decimation of indigenous peoples in every region of the world (estimates unavailable).

This is obviously a partial, not a comprehensive, list. A complete list would require far more research into this field, and would include more limited 'holocausts' such as the French in Algeria, the Americans in Vietnam, the Russians in Chechnya, the Japanese in China – in short, an entire history of conflict and war. I am grateful to John Churchill for his contribution to this holocaust research and for helping me understand more clearly its relationship to the themes of this book.

[13] Kurt Mobius quoted in Daniel Jonah Goldhagen, *Hitler's Willing Executioners: Ordinary Germans and the Holocaust* (New York: Knopf, 1997), p. 179.

[14] David Brooks, 'What Price Globalization? Managing Costs at Microsoft', in *Translating Into Success*, ed. Robert C. Sprung (American Translators Association Scholarly Monograph Series Volume XI).

[15] 'Learn to listen', for example, is one of the 'twelve essential rules of negotiation' in Leigh Steinerg, *Winning With Integrity* (New York: Villard, 1998).

[16] Nelson Mandela, *Long Walk To Freedom* (Boston: Little Brown, 1995), p. 19.

[17] This list is a modified version of one that appears in Ronald S. Kraybill with Robert A. Evans and Alice Frazer Evans, *Peace Skills: Manual for Community Mediators* (San Francisco: Jossey-Bass, 2001), p. 88.

[18] For a full version of Tutu's commentary on this and other aspects of the Commission's work, the final report is available

from the commission or visit
http://www.polity.org.za/polity/govdocs/commissions/1998/trc/index.htm.

[19] Jimmy Carter reported in 'This week with George Stephanopolous', 13 April 2008, abcnews.go.com/ThisWeek/Story?id=4641038&page=1.

[20] Jimmy Carter, 'Pariah Diplomacy', *New York Times*, 28 April 2008, p. A27.

[21] Poll cited in ibid.

4. Geo-Partnering

[1] 'U.S. and Cuba Work Together on Storms,' Marc Lacey, New York Times, August 20, 2009.

[2] See http://www.gaia.com/quotes/topics/collaboration.

[3] From his news conference at the G20 conference, cited in *Newsweek*, 13 April 2009, p. 19.

[4] Richard N. Haass, *The Opportunity: America's Moment to Alter History's Course*, (New York: Public Affairs, 2005), pp. 199–200.

[5] To find out the results of this meeting and the impact of this organization, please go to www.ticahealth.org.

[6] J. F. Rischard, *High Noon: Twenty Issues and Twenty Years to Solve Them* (New York: Basic Books, 2002), p. 66.

[7] From a speech delivered at the Carter Center in Atlanta Georgia. January 2002. http://www.cartercenter.org/news/documents/doc81.html

[8] Dick Filgate quoted in D'Arcy Doran, 'Women Claim Victory in Chevron Oil Terminal Takeover', Associated Press, 19 July 2002.

[9] Interviews with the author, October 2008.

[10] 'Make Trade Fair', report issued by Oxfam International, April 2002. For more information, go to http://www.oxfam.org/en/campaigns/trade/rigged_rules.

[11] 'Who Really Pays to Help US Farmers?', Paul Blustein, *Washington Post*, 6 May 2002.

12 Jeffrey D. Sachs, 'Homegrown Aid', *New York Times*, 9 April 2009, p. A23.

13 C. K. Prahalad, *The Fortune at the Bottom of the Pyramid* (Upper Saddle River, N.J.: Wharton School, 2006).

14 Like other phrases in this field – developed and underdeveloped, asset-rich and asset-poor, etc. – 'haves' and 'have-nots' is misleading. Many of the so-called 'have-nots' in fact have a lot of assets. To describe them in such polarized terms says more about the poverty of our language than the poverty of their lives. This does not mean that some of the 'have-nots' are not actually destitute and in urgent need of support. It does mean that we need to witness them in the fullness of who they are, not just through the lenses of income levels or material comforts.

15 Simanis, Erik, and Stuart L. Hart (2008), *The Base of the Pyramid Protocol: Toward Next Generation BoP Strategy*, Center for Sustainable Global Enterprise, Cornell University. p. 23.

16 Ibid., pp 23ff.

17 Shree Krishna Padre, an Ashoka Fellow, is profiled in *Leading Social Entrepreneurs, Ashoka Fellows Elected 1999 and 2000*. For more information, contact www.ashoka.org or www.changemakers.org.

18 This argument is fully developed and beautifully expressed in René Dubos, *The Wooing of Earth* (New York: Scribner, 1980).

19 Interview with the author, November 2008.

20 For more information, go to www.southsouthnorth.org.

21 Interview with the author, November 2008.

22 Interview with the author, September 2008.

23 The Report of the Commission, called the 'Brundtland Report' after its visionary chairperson, Gro Harlem Brundtland, was a turning point and is worth reading to understand how recently we as a species became aware of this issue which may determine the human future. United Nations, *Report of the World Commission on Environment and Development*,

General Assembly Resolution 42/187, 11 December 1987.

[24] Bjørn Lomborg quoted in 'Environmentalists have it backward', *International Herald Tribune*, 27 August 2002.

[25] Profile of Kofi Annan, *Time Magazine*, 26 August 2002.

[26] Paul Hawken, Amory Lovins, Hunter Lovins, *Natural Capitalism* (Boston: Little Brown, 1999).

[27] Peter Senge et al., *The Necessary Revolution* (New York: Doubleday, 2008).

[28] There is a vast literature on this topic. For a credible overview, see *The Military's Impact on the Environment: A Neglected Aspect of the Sustainable Development Debate, A Briefing Paper for States and Non-Governmental Organisations*, International Peace Bureau, Geneva, August 2002.

[29] Based on the continuously updated figures provided by www.costofwar.com.

[30] Please consult the research by the Strategic Foresight Group in Mumbai, India, which has conducted detailed analyses of the costs of both conflicts. See www.strategicforesight.com.

[31] *Washington Post*, 19 May 2009.

[32] Nick Wadhams, 'A Massacre in a Kenyan Church', *Time Magazine*, 1 January 2008.

[33] Daniel Opande reported in 'Liberian Rebels Still Terrorizing, U.N. Finds', *Los Angeles Times*, 9 November 2003.

[34] Abraham McLaughlin, 'Africa's peace seekers: Lazaro Sumbeiywo', *Christian Science Monitor*, 9 December 2005.

[35] These statements are a synopsis of my conversation with Hekmat Karzai; his speech at the conference; and Hekmat Karzai and Julian Lindley-French, 'Listening to Afghans', *Afghanistan Times*, 19 November 2007, p. 29.

[36] Kai Eide quoted in Kirk Semple, 'Official Calls for Sensitivity to Afghan Demands', *New York Times*, 7 December 2008.

[37] Stanley Mc Chrystal reported in Carlotta Gall and Taimoor Shah, 'Afghans Recall Airstrike Horror, and Fault U.S.', *New York Times*, 15 May 2009, and 'U.S. Report Finds Airstrike

Errors in Afghan Deaths', 3 June 2009.

[38] Martin Schweitzer quoted in David Rohde, 'Army Enlists Anthropology in War Zones', *New York Times*, 8 August 2007.

[39] Ibid.

[40] Interview with the author May, 2008.

[41] An internal memorandum written by Ambassador Hennig for the East West Institute, September 2008.

[42] Manuscript: David Kilcullen, *The Accidental Guerilla*, p. 49.

[43] Daniel Gavron, *Holy Land Mosaic: Stories of Cooperation and Coexistence Between Palestinians and Israelis* (Lanham: Rowan and Littlefield, 2008), p. 195.

[44] Interview with the author in Jerusalem, April 2002.

[45] Interview with the author in Jerusalem, April 2002.

[46] Medea Benjamin, Andrea Freeman, Sarah Miles, *Bridging the Global Gap: A Handbook to Linking Citizens of the First and Third Worlds* (Washington, DC: Seven Locks Press, 2005).

Conclusion: Global Intelligence

[1] For a single volume that introduces this literature, the best starting point is Mansour Javidan et al., *The Global Mindset* (Amsterdam; Oxford: Elsevier JAI, 2007).

[2] The physiology of the brain is more complex, of course. The left brain, which is associated with logic and calculation, performs more 'rational' functions. The right brain, which is associated with artistic activity and imagination, is associated more with emotive responses. For a fascinating look at this subject, see Daniel H. Pink, *A Whole New Mind* (New York: Penguin), 2005.

[3] Mansour Javidan, speech at the Center for Integrative Leadership, University of Minnesota, 3 October 2008.

[4] Tara Parker-Pope, 'One-Eyed Invader in the Bedroom', *New York Times*, 16 September 2008. For more information, contact Leonard H. Epstein, Professor of Pediatrics and Social and

Preventive Medicine at the School of Medicine and Biomedical Science at the State University of New York in Buffalo.

5   For further information, please visit www.acommonword.com.

6   Jason Hill reported in Walter Truett Anderson, 'The Case for Global Citizenship', Pacific News Service, 13 June 2003.

7   For more information, go to http://en.wikipedia.org/wiki/Han_Chinese.

8   Jeffrey Garten quoted in 'Asia's Recovery Highlights China's Ascendance,' Nelson D. Schwartz, *New York Times*, 23 August, 2009

9   Nelson D. Schwartz, 'Asia's Recovery Highlights China's Ascendancy', *New York Times*, 24 July 2009; Jeffrey E. Garten, 'American Still Rules', *Newsweek*, 3 July 2009.

10 Charles Krauthammer, 'Clinton and Co. deferred Iraq crisis', *Daily Camera*, 15 February 2003.

11 Zbigniew Brzezinski, *The Choice* (New York: 2004).

12 Jeffrey Sachs, *Common Wealth: Economics for a Crowded Planet* (London: Penguin, 2009), p. 289.

13 Vaclav Havel, *To The Castle and Back* (New York: Vintage, 2008).

14 Interview with the author in Jerusalem, April 2002.

15 Unfortunately, I cannot locate the particular publication in which this interview appeared.

16 For more information, go to abrahampath.org or http://www.armscontrol.org/factsheets/Nuclearweaponswhoh aswhat October 2007.

17 For more information, go to www.drinking-water.org.

18 Interview with the author in Boulder, Colorado, August 2009.

19 Lester Brown, 'Telling the ecological truth', *Ode Magazine*, June/July 2009, p. 24.

20 For more about MVP, go to http://www.millenniumvillages.org/; or see Jeffrey Sachs, op. cit., pp. 238ff.

21 Larry Brilliant and Daniel Goleman, 'On Compassionate Capitalism', *Kosmos Magazine*, Fall/Winter 2008.

22 Jeffrey Sachs, op. cit., p. 320.

23 Marilyn Hamilton, *Integral City: Evolutionary Intelligences for the Human Hive* (Gabriola Island, BC: New Society Publishers, 2008).

24 For more information on the 'fair trade' movement, contact the World Fair Trade Organization (www.wfto.com), the Fair Trade Federation (www.fairtradefederation.org), Trans Fair, www.transfairusa.org or the many organizations listed at www.wiserearth.org.

25 Comments by Mansour Javidan at the Center for Integrative Leadership, University of Minnesota, 5 October 2008.

26 An Interview with Dr Angel Cabrera, President, Thunderbird, the Garvin School of International Management, 'Emphasizing Global Citizenship for Business Leaders', in *International Educator* (Jan–Feb 2005), pp. 14–17.

27 The Golden Rule as expressed in the major faiths of humankind:

> Do unto others as you would have others do unto you. *Christianity*
>
> What is hateful to you, do not do to your fellow man. *Judaism*
>
> No one is a believer until he desires for his brother that which he desires for himself. *Islam*
>
> Do not do unto others what would cause you pain if done unto you. *Hinduism*
>
> Hurt not others in ways that you yourself would find hurtful. *Buddhism*
>
> Regard your neighbour's gain as your gain and your neighbour's loss as your own loss. *Taoism*

About the Author

As President of Mediators Foundation, which he founded over twenty years ago, Mark Gerzon has launched scores of projects that have advanced the field of global citizenship. He has also worked with a wide variety of organizations, including the US Congress, multinational corporations, and the United Nations. The author of numerous books, including the recent *Leading Through Conflict* (Harvard Business School Press), he lectures and conducts leadership workshops throughout the world.

For four decades, Gerzon has been involved in global affairs – first as a student (he lived in families in seven different cultures during his year with the International Honors Program); next as a citizen diplomat (he worked for several years bringing together Soviet and American civic leaders to help end the Cold War); then as a journalist (he co-founded *WorldPaper*, a 'global newspaper' which reached a circulation of 1.5 million in five languages); and more recently as a leadership consultant and UN mediator.

In 2006, he founded the Conflict Transformation Collaborative, a network of peace-builders from around the world which connects more than one hundred grassroots mediators. He is also designing an interactive workshop 'The Global Citizen Experience' based on this book, which provides citizens, old and young, with an opportunity to raise their global intelligence and identify how they can uniquely serve the earth.

For more information about these initiatives, go to www.mediatorsfoundtion.org.

Index